62365

Central Bible College Library
Springfield, Missouri

pages were glued together

THE CHANGED POLITICAL THOUGHT OF THE NEGRO, 1915-1940

Central Bible College Library
Springfield, Missouri

The Changed Political Thought of the Negro

1915 — 1940

by ELBERT LEE TATUM

With a Foreword by Lawrence A. Davis

62365

GREENWOOD PRESS, PUBLISHERS
WESTPORT, CONNECTICUT

Central Bible College Library
Springfield, Missouri

Library of Congress Cataloging in Publication Data

Tatum, Elbert Lee.
The changed political thought of the Negro, 1915-1940.

Reprint of the ed. published by Exposition Press, New York.
Bibliography: p.
1. Negroes--Politics and suffrage. 2. Political affiliation--United States. I. Title.
JK2275.N4T3 1974 329 73-16739
ISBN 0-8371-7217-9

Copyright 1951 by Elbert Lee Tatum

All rights reserved including the right of reproduction in whole or in part in any form

Originally published in 1951 by Exposition Press, New York

Reprinted with the permission of Exposition Press, Inc.

Reprinted in 1974 by Greenwood Press, a division of Williamhouse-Regency Inc.

Library of Congress Catalogue Card Number 73-16739

ISBN 0-8371-7217-9

Printed in the United States of America

Dedicated to the memory of my mother, Alice Smiley Tatum, because better than anyone else whom I know she represented the ideal in love, patience, helpfulness, and aspiration.

E. L. T.

FOREWORD

The professor in the small college who possesses scholarly ambitions and capability, and impelling urges to enhance his field of interest, finds his path fraught with handicaps and odds. Most often an excessive teaching-load assignment, the unavailability of materials, and woefully inadequate funds preclude any attempt at producing materials for publication. This situation is acutely prevalent in colleges exclusively for Negroes.

Therefore, it is particularly notable that Dr. Elbert Lee Tatum has found the time and resources to produce so significant a work as *The Changed Political Thought of the Negro, 1915-1940*.

It is not just another book. Upon the announcement of any book on the Negro, one naturally begins to question the need, for he at once thinks of the meritorious and exhaustive editions of Brawley, DuBois, Johnson, Locke, Williams, Woodson; Franklin, Myrdal, and Frazier's recent *The Negro in the United States*.

However, these have only given categorical and routine treatment of the Negro's role and importance as a participant in the political affairs of the United States. Dr. Tatum has brought us up to date on the Negro as an active political factor in America. He presents not only a political history of the Negro, but an analytical and definitive interpretation of his importance as a participant in political affairs in America with infinite patience and intimate understanding. He also delineates the changes in the Negro's political thinking.

Dr. Tatum has not wandered about into bypaths and excursions over the whole range of Negro life and history in the United States. He has stayed with his subject all the way. He has not become emotional or biased. He has simply found the truth and revealed it as he has discovered it, enhancing its appeal, of course, with brilliant illumination. He has remained consistently in character as the disinterested, objective scholar.

The work appears at a most propitious time in the history of the Negro and the evolution of American democracy. The Negro, especially in the South, is just becoming fully politically articulate, and his loyalty is being sought by parties and by individuals on every hand. At the same time the impact of world affairs forces America to accelerate her rate of accepting Negroes as first-class citizens, while the Negro wisely uses politics as one of his vehicles of advancement.

Dr. Tatum has made a distinct and unique contribution in this volume, which, I predict, will find wide-scale use throughout American institutions in the fields of history and political science.

LAWRENCE A. DAVIS, *President,*
Agriculture, Normal and
Mechanical College,
Pine Bluff, Arkansas

PREFACE

The purpose of this study is to determine why Negroes in the United States have changed their traditional political allegiance from the Republican party. A correct appraisal of the degree and extent of the change requires an inquiry into and an examination of the causes of his tie to the Republican party since the party was first organized. By such an examination and inquiry we are able to see to what the Negro was loyal for over three generations. This study sets as a part of its objective an evaluation of the forces which played a role in producing the change which was everywhere manifested in 1940.

Was the change the result of inherent weakness in the policies and programs of the Republican party? Did the change result from serious thought and judgment on the part of the Negro relative to limited participation in the Republican councils? Did the Negro change parties in an effort to raise his status as an American citizen? How far was the Republican indifference, and tacit acquiescence with the southern Democrats, responsible for the Negro's change of party politics? How far was the Democratic bid, the deference and considerations shown Negroes recently, responsible for wooing the Negro from the Republican party? Finally, did the Negro, as a result of migration to the North, change his traditional belief in the divinity of the Republican label to a belief that men and measures were far more valuable than the labels which the men wore?

The writer's interest in this problem was aroused while a graduate student in political science at the University of Illinois,

1932-1933. Some data were collected at that time to prepare a thesis on "The History and Organization of the Republican Party." The subject was changed for several reasons but those data collected were preserved and from time to time others were acquired. The written classroom reports of several of the writer's students at both Langston University and Morgan State College were means of conserving his energies for the greater problems lying ahead. However, before the incorporation of any expression in this book, it was verified; all claims and contentions are supported by evidence.

The newspapers referred to were made available to the writer by their publishers, excepting *The Cleveland Plain Dealer* and the *Pittsburgh Courier,* which were studied at the Library of Congress in Washington, 1943-1944. The writer wishes to thank Miss Olive M. Diggs, editor of the *Chicago Bee*; Mr. C. A. Franklin, editor of the *Kansas City Call;* Mr. J. H. Singlestacke, editor of the *Chicago Defender*; Mr. J. E. Mitchell, editor, the *St. Louis Argus;* Mr. L. W. Werner of the *New York Age;* Mr. Carl Murphy, editor of the *Baltimore Afro-American;* Reverend C. P. Powell, editor of the *Amsterdam News,* and Mr. Roscoe Dungee of the *Black Dispatch* for permitting him access to their newspaper files.

The members of the staffs in the libraries of Chicago—the Newberry, the John Crerar, the Chicago Public, especially the George Cleveland Hall Branch, the University of Chicago, Northwestern University, and Loyola University—have generally been generous in help and patience. To all of them the writer expresses his sincere thanks.

A debt of gratitude is owed to members of the faculty of history in the Graduate School of Loyola University, Chicago, which is greater than the writer can repay. They saved him from many errors in both fact and judgment. Their excellent guidance, their seemingly unlimited wisdom, their endless patience, and, above all, the goodness of their hearts were a constant challenge and motivation to the writer.

Thanks are also due to Mr. Ernest A. Greene and Mr. Joseph D. Bibb, both attorneys at law of Chicago, Illinois, and Mr. Claude A. Barnett, Director of the Associated Negro Press, Inc., Chicago, Illinois, for permission to reproduce their respective letters to the author in the Appendixes of this book.

Finally the patience, the sacrifice and encouragement of my wife, Ola Mae Tatum, was a contributing factor in this study. Her unselfishness added to her other divinely endowed qualities gave the writer inspiration, renewed determination and resolution to continue the study. Without her and the consolation found in her devotion the book might not have been completed.

Whatever imperfections, weaknesses, and limitations this work contains are the author's alone. Since the errors are neither known nor willed the author finds some consolation in the expression of Justice Oliver Wendell Holmes, "Every year, if not every day, we have to wager our salvation upon some prophecy based upon imperfect knowledge." Thus the writer says with Chaucer's Squire,

> Hold me excused, if I say ought amiss,
> My aim is good, and lo, my tale is this.

Contents

INTRODUCTION

The attitude one possesses in approaching this problem is exceedingly important. Anyone who approaches this subject with a fixed opinion about the Negro, whether favorable or unfavorable, is likely to find himself confusing what the truth is with what he wants the truth to be. It is obvious how such a mentality would prevent an objective and scientific analysis of the data, thereby rendering the production not a work of science. One of the first requirements of the scientist is the possession of a correct mental set—a mind open to truths whether bitter or sweet.

It is not the objective of this study to write the history of the Negro in the United States; such has been brilliantly done by several persons.[1] The objective of this study is to determine the extent to which the political thought of the Negro has been modified in the period 1915-1940, the causes of this modification,

1 Benjamin G. Brawley, *A Short History of the American Negro,* The Macmillan Company, New York, 1939. W. E. B. DuBois, *The Negro,* Henry Holt and Company, New York, 1915. Charles S. Johnson, *The Negro in American Civilization,* Henry Holt and Company, New York, 1930. Allain L. Locke, *The New Negro,* Associates in Negro Folk Education, Washington, D.C., 1937. George S. Merriam, *The Negro and the Nation,* Henry Holt and Company, New York, 1906. George W. Williams, *History of the Negro Race in America,* G. P. Putnam's Sons, New York, 1880. Carter G. Woodson, *The Negro in Our History,* The Associated Publishers, Washington, D. C., 1945. John Hope Franklin, *From Slavery to Freedom,* Alfred A. Knopf, New York, 1949.

and its consequences. If this undertaking is important, its importance lies to a considerable extent in the answer to two questions. First, what role did the Negro play prior to 1915? And secondly, does it make any difference to the whole nation what his thinking has been in the period under consideration—1915-1940? The answer to the first of these questions involves consideration of the influences and forces which were acting upon him prior to 1915, since it is a well-established fact that patterns of behavior are not isolated, completed entities in themselves, but are dependent and coordinated. The answer to the second question involves an analysis of our concept of majority rule, for if his thought and consequently his action make no difference in the political affairs of this country, then the United States is not governed democratically but dictatorially. Any admission contrary to this is also contrary to the democratic way of life.

The reader's attention is called to the limited nature of this study, limited by time to a twenty-five year period, and limited in scope to one aspect of the Negro's behavior, namely, political.

THE CHANGED POLITICAL THOUGHT OF THE NEGRO, 1915-1940

CHAPTER I

The Political Significance of Negro Migration to the North, 1915-1940

The political role which the Negro has played, either directly or indirectly, is older than the nation itself. Notwithstanding the claims of several writers of history that Negroes first came to America in 1619 as slaves, an increasing number of historians have been able to show by use of documents and the findings of anthropologists, geologists and philologists, that Negroes came to the New World much earlier than 1619 and at least some of them were not slaves.[1] Woodson believes that Pedro Alonso Niño, a pilot of one of Columbus' ships, was a Negro and declares,

> In the discovery of the Pacific Ocean, Balboa carried with him thirty Negroes including Nuflo de Olana. In the conquest of Mexico, Cortez was accompanied by

1 Melville J. Herskovits, *The Myth of the Negro Past,* Harper and Brothers, New York, 1943, 293.

> a Negro . . . Negroes assisted in the conquest of Guatemala, and the conquest of Chile, Peru, and Venezuela. Negroes accompanied De Allyon in 1526 in his expedition from the Florida peninsula northward and figured in the settlement of San Miguel near what is now Jamestown, Virginia. They accompanied Narváez in his ill-fated expedition in 1527 and continued with Cabeza de Vaca, his successor, through what is now the northern part of the United States. They went with Alarcon and Coronado in the conquest of Mexico.[2]

The above citation puts Negroes among the earliest explorers of this continent and nothing in the citation indicates that their condition was different from the condition of other adventurers. It is the belief of some recent writers that the twenty Negroes who landed at Jamestown were bound out as indentured servants.[3] An enactment of the Virginia legislature in 1661 lends support to the proposition when it declared that Negroes "were incapable of making satisfaction by *addition of* time for their loss in running away."[4] Why "addition of time" if Negroes were already slaves? This fact is revealing because it shows Negroes were bound out for limited duration prior to 1661 and that lawmakers were required to enact measures to protect those who had contracted for their services. The reports of the committee of the Council of Burgesses contain extensive discussions by its members over the question of

2 Carter G. Woodson, *The Negro in Our History,* (eighth edition), Associated Publishers, Washington, D.C., 1945, 58-59 (hereafter, Woodson's *Negro in Our History*).

3 W. E. B. DuBois, *The Negro,* Henry Holt and Company, New York, 1915, 186. Also, Woodson's *Negro in Our History*, 57.

4 William Waller Herring, *Statutes at Large, A Collection of Laws of Virginia from the First Session of Its Legislature in 1619,* Richmond, 1819, II, 26.

slavery.[5] The number of laws enacted in an effort to regulate every aspect of slavery gives some notion of the political significance of the subject.[6]

1. Colonial Times

In the early years of American colonial history white indentured servants were sufficient for the labor demands. For that cause Negro slavery was for many years stagnant, or it grew quite slowly. However, in 1688 England ceased to export indentured servants, thereby creating an instant need for more Negro slaves. Accordingly, the number increased from an estimated 58,850 in 1715 to 501,000 in 1775.[7] When the first census was taken by the United States in 1790 there were 757,000 slaves in the country in a total population of 3,929,214.[8] Due in part to increased demands for more slaves from Africa and the West Indies, several states of Europe fitted out ships with which large numbers of slaves were brought to the American shores. By 1800 there were 893,041 slaves in the North American colonies.[9]

The political importance of the slaves is not contingent upon their number alone. In fact their political importance lies more in their quality than in quantity, for if they were subhuman beings incapable of civilization morally, a number of slaves was no different from any other number of valuable things which their owners possessed, such as animals or farm

5 W. O. Blake, *The Political History of Slavery in the United States*, Columbus, Ohio, 1857, 369-79. (Compiled from source material published and sold exclusively by subscription. Hereafter Blake's *Political History*.)

6 *Ibid.*, 370-88.

7 *Ibid.*, 378-88.

8 *First Census*, 1790, Census Bureau, Massachusetts, Government Printing Office, Washington, D.C., 1908, 8.

9 Blake, *Political History*, 430.

implements. But to admit that slaves were human beings with minds capable of development was to admit a degree of actual or potential political importance not associated with animals. Human beings in a democratic process are counted to determine the number of representatives to be elected to the assemblies, how justice is to be administered, and the method of regulating the civil, political and economic policies of the nation. Indeed, the effort to fix status upon the Negro, both free and slave, brought forth many heated discussions in every colonial assembly after 1621.[10]

The discussions centered around such questions as: whether the slave should be regarded as person or property; whether manumission should follow conversion; whether slaves could own land; whether free Negroes might own slaves; who and what determined the status of the offspring; what was the relation between master and slave; what should the penalty be for intermarriage; what was the status of children when one parent is colored and the other white, or one free and the other slave?

Prior to 1662, slavery was not hereditary. It was in this year, however, that Virginia initiated such a system, and all of the colonies thereafter followed suit: Maryland, 1663; Massachusetts, 1698; Connecticut and New Jersey, 1704; Pennsylvania and New York, 1706; South Carolina, 1712; Rhode Island, 1728; and North Carolina, 1741.[11] This tends to emphasize the significance of the Negro in the deliberation of the legislative bodies.

More laws were enacted which dealt with the Negro during colonial times than any one other subject; everything from

10 Richard Hildreth, *Despotism in America, An Inquiry into the Slave-holding System*, John Jewett and Company, Cleveland, 1854, 71-72 (hereafter Hildreth's *Despotism*).

11 *Ibid.*, 177-219.

hereditary slavery to prohibition of slavery was discussed at length.[12]

One would be led too far afield from the immediate undertaking if he followed the arguments supporting and denouncing the system through all the colonial assemblies even though they were interesting and informative. It is sufficient for the purpose here to note that there were able men on both sides who kept the issue of slavery alive, some going so far as to invoke the sacred Scriptures to lend support to their claims.

2. *Importance During Revolutionary Period*

The Revolutionary philosophy, with emphasis upon freedom, liberty, consent of the governed, and independence during the contest for independence, led several Negroes to participate in that war. Their willingness to suffer and die for such lofty ideals were among the causes for much discussion in the postwar period. The disposition of territories belonging to the colonies recently confederated as partially independent states became a subject of solicitude in the states and Congress. By the terms of their charters some of the states had an indefinite extension westward, limited only by the power of the grantor. Some of the charters conflicted with each other where the same territory was included within the limits of two or more totally distinct colonies. That situation created many problems when the expenses of war began to bear heavily upon the resources of some of the states. Those without territory in the West claimed that their advantages in the expected triumph would be less than those states with western lands.

Massachusetts, Connecticut, New York, Virginia, North Carolina, and Georgia laid claims to vast dominions beyond their boundaries, while New Hampshire (save in the section

12 Blake, *Political History*, 380-83.

now making the state of Vermont), Rhode Island, New Jersey, Maryland, Delaware, and South Carolina possessed no such dominions with which to meet their war debts. The latter urged, with obvious justice, a surrender of those unequal advantages to the Federal government, that is, all the lands within the territorial limits but outside of the natural boundaries of the several states. That land, under the suggestion of the "landless states," was to be held by Congress in trust for the common benefit of all the states, and the proceeds therefrom were to be employed in satisfying the debts and liabilities of the Confederation. This suggestion was ultimately responded to with reservations: Virginia reserved a sufficiency beyond the Ohio to furnish bounties promised to her Revolutionary officers and soldiers; Connecticut demanded a western reserve simply because her charter provided for it; Massachusetts required five million acres in New York to be reserved as Massachusetts' territory because her colonial charter provided for it.[13]

The cessions were made after the close of the Revolutionary War. One of the duties imposed upon the Continental Congress which held its session in Philadelphia was the framing of an act or ordinance for the government of the vast dominion which had been committed to its care and disposal. Congress placed the duty of disposing the territory in the hands of a committee consisting of Thomas Jefferson of Virginia, Chairman; S. Chase of Maryland, and Mr. Howell of Rhode Island. In due time the committee reported a plan of government of the western territory which embraced several of the slave states. This plan contemplated the division of the territory into seventeen states, eight below the parallel of the Falls of the

13 Albert Bushnell Hart and Edward Channing, editors, *American History Leaflets, Colonial and Constitutional,* Parker B. Simmons Company, Inc., New York, 1896, Number 22, 1-37.

Ohio and nine above it. Among other rules reported by the Jefferson committee were the following:

> After the year 1800 of the Christian era, there shall be neither slavery nor involuntary servitude in any of the *said* states, otherwise than in punishment of crime, whereof the party shall have been convicted to be personally guilty.[14]

As soon as the report was finished Mr. Spaight of North Carolina made a motion to strike out the paragraph dealing with slavery, and Mr. Read of South Carolina seconded the motion. Mr. Howell of the House asked for a vote upon the motion which he put as follows: "Shall the words moved to be struck out stand?" The question was lost, the words were struck out altogether, six states voted "aye" while three voted "nay"; fifteen members voted for and six against Jefferson's proposition.[15] Under the terms of the Articles of Confederation, nine states were required to carry a proposition. Since this requirement was not met, the comprehensive exclusion of slavery from the Federal territory was defeated. The ordinance, after undergoing several amendments, was approved, all delegates but those from the South voting in the affirmative.

In 1787 while the last Continental Congress was sitting in New York, simultaneously with the convention at Philadelphia which framed the Federal Constitution, the question of the government of the territory was again taken up. A bill was submitted by the chairman, Nathan Dane of Massachusetts, which embodied with modifications many of the provisions

14 *Miscellaneous Documents of the House of Representatives for the Second Session of the Forty-seventh Congress,* 1882-1883, Government Printing Office, Washington, D.C., Volume XIX, 151-53.

15 *Ibid.,* 152.

originally drafted and reported by the Jefferson committee. There were six articles of perpetual compact in the bill, the last of them as follows: "There shall be neither slavery nor involuntary servitude in the said territory otherwise than in punishment of crime whereof the parties shall be duly convicted.[16] This law prohibited slavery in the Northwest Territory, which contained a larger area than the slave states of the South. The biggest question in considering the western land loomed around slavery.

One does not need an unusual mentality to be able to see how Negroes as slaves played a politically important role in American colonial history. The deliberation, discussions and enactment centering around them when the Ordinance of 1784 and that of 1787 were under consideration lend emphasis to the point. Those who led the discussions might have been motivated by economic and religious considerations; nevertheless, it required political manipulations and strategy to get their points over. The inescapable deduction is that the slave was politically significant or else the lawmakers unwisely employed their best talent for a considerable portion of the time.

3. The Constitutional Convention

In 1787, the convention of delegates from the several states was legally assembled at Philadelphia to revise the Articles of Confederation. The result of their labors was the formation of a Constitution for the United States. Eleven states sent fifty-five of their most illustrous citizens—men highly distinguished for talents, character, practical knowledge and public service. Eighteen of those members were at the same time delegates to the Continental Congress, and there were only

16 *Ibid.*, 156.

twelve who had not sat at some time in that body.[17] One ot the first major problems to be settled was the rule of apportionment. What should be the number of representatives in the first branch of the legislature? Ought the number from each state to be fixed or should it increase with the increase of population? Ought population alone be the basis of apportionment, or should property be taken into account? Those were some of the questions to be answered before much could be done to establish a more perfect union.

It is plain that whatever rule might be adopted, no apportionment founded upon population could be made until an enumeration of the inhabitants was taken. The number of representatives was at first fixed at sixty-five, but in establishing a rule for future apportionment great diversity of opinion was expressed.

In 1787, slavery existed in every state other than Massachusetts; however, the great mass of slaves were in the southern states. The southern states insisted on representation according to number, bond and free, while the northern states insisted on representation according to the number of free persons only. Each point was forcibly urged by able representatives. For example, Mr. Patterson of New Jersey regarded slaves only as property, and pointed out that if they were not represented in the state, why should they be in the general government? "They are not allowed to vote, why should they be represented?" James Wilson of Pennsylvania asked, "Are they admitted as citizens? Why not on equality with citizens? Are they admitted as property, then why is not other property admitted into the computation?"[18]

17 W. Hickey, editor, *State Papers, Public Documents and Other Sources of Political and Statististical Information,* T. K. and P. G. Collins, Philadelphia, 1847, 191.

18 Blake, *Political History,* 394.

Members of the convention from both sections of the Union, who saw that neither extreme could be carried, responded to the suggestion of the aged Benjamin Franklin to compromise by counting the whole number of free citizens and three fifths of all others. Before the vote could be taken on the report, a proviso was moved and agreed to that direct taxes should be in proportion to representation. Subsequently a proposition was moved to count three fifths of the slaves in estimating taxes and making taxation the basis of representation. The latter proposition was discussed pro and con relative to its merits. The discussions finally revived opposition to the apportionment of representatives according to the three-fifths ratio.

Some of the best statesmen severely denounced slavery; for example, Mr. King of Massachusetts declared that he could never agree to let slaves be imported without limitation, and be represented in legislature. "Either slaves should not be represented or exports should be taxable." Gouverneur Morris of Pennsylvania pronounced slavery "a nefarious institution. It is the curse of heaven on the states where it prevails." Mr. Mason of Virginia declared,

> Slavery discourages arts and manufacture. The poor despise labor when performed by slaves. They prevent the immigration of whites, who really enrich and strengthen a country.[19]

The comments of a few who defended slavery should also be mentioned, for they show how keen was the clash of opinions over the question. Mr. Ellsworth of Connecticut said:

19 G. Hunt and J. B. Scott, editors, *Debates in the Federal Convention of 1787 Which Formed the Constitution of the United States of America,* Oxford University Press, New York, 1920, 201-26.

> Let every state import what it pleases. The morality or wisdom of slavery is a consideration belonging to the states. What enriches a part enriches the whole and the states are the best judges of their particular interests.[20]

Mr. C. Pinckney of South Carolina said, "South Carolina can never receive the plan if it [the three-fifths ratio] prohibits the slave trade."[21] Delegates from South Carolina and Georgia repeated the declaration that if the slave trade were prohibited, their states would not adopt the Constitution. General Gerry of Massachusetts thought the members of the convention should have nothing to do with the conduct of the states as to slavery, but declared "they should be careful not to give any sanction to it."[22]

In the debates as reported by James Madison, the Negro and the slavery question were constantly brought before the convention. Slavery was a national institution and there were friends and foes of the institution in all sections of the country. Anyone who reads the proceedings and debates cannot escape the impression that Negroes, both slave and free, were an item of unusual political importance.

4. *The Constitution*

The references in the Constitution to the Negro, directly or indirectly, slaves or freemen, tend to emphasize their political importance. Among its provisions which refer especially to the Negro or to the subject of slavery are the following:

20 *Ibid.*, 442.
21 *Ibid.*, 443.
22 *Ibid.*, 440.

Preamble:

> We the people of the United States, in order to form a more perfect union, establish justice, insure domestic tranquillity, . . . promote the general welfare, and secure the blessings of liberty . . .

Article I, Section 2:

> Representatives and direct taxes shall be apportioned among the several States which may be included within this Union according to their respective numbers, which shall be determined by adding to the whole number of free persons, including those bound to servitude for a term of years, and excluding Indians not taxed, three-fifths of all other persons.

Section 9:

> The migration or importation of such persons as any of the States now existing shall think proper to admit shall not be prohibited by the Congress prior to the year 1808, but a tax or duty may be imposed . . . not exceeding ten dollars for each person.

Article IV, Section 2:

> The citizens of each State shall be entitled to all the privileges of citizens in the several States. . . .
>
> No person held to service or labor in one State, under the laws thereof, escaping into another shall in conse-

> quence of any law or regulation therein, be discharged from such service or labor, but shall be delivered up on claim of the party to whom such service or labor may be due.

One notices the absence of the words "slave" or "slavery" in the document. Mr. Madison, who was a leading and observant member of the convention, and who took notes of its daily proceedings, affirms that this silence was designed—the convention being unwilling for the Constitution to recognize property in human beings.[23] In passages where slaves are presumed to be contemplated, they are uniformly designated as "persons," never as property. In a state supposedly based upon Christian principles the fathers of the Constitution were ashamed to let the world know that such an institution as slavery had their sanction. Surely some of the Constitutional fathers were proud of their phenomenal achievements but there were an increasing number who believed the achievement to be of temporary duration. One of the reasons for the belief was the question of slavery.[24]

Time devoted to discussing slavery and slaves in the Constitutional Convention and the amount of space given to the subject in the instrument itself are indicative of the political importance of the slave.

5. *The Period 1787-1865*

From the time the Constitution was framed in 1787 to the time Lincoln issued the Emancipation Proclamation of 1862, no subject received more attention from the lawmakers and

23 *Ibid.*, 469. "The reasons of duty are without basis as slaves are not like merchandise, consumed, etc.," was his argument.

24 *Ibid.*, 130-36. See Luther Martin's discussion on national government and the sovereignty of states.

the administrations than slavery. The judiciary of both states and federal governments at times were called upon to decide controversial issues in regard to certain aspects of the subject.[25] The major political considerations centered around the following: prohibition of slavery; slavery in new states; fugitive slave laws; circulation of anti-slavery publications in the mails; the Webster, Clay, Benton versus Buchanan and Talmadge debates; the annexation of Texas; the Compromise of 1850; the Kansas-Nebraska Bill; Congressional proceedings about the affairs in Kansas; and the Dred Scott case. Fortunately for the writer, such topics have received excellent treatment at the hands of many experts, which appear in a number of general and special works.[26]

The welfare of the United States, apart from any danger from without, and more especially the welfare of the slave states, called ever louder for executive, legislative and judicial interference. Sensible to the evil of slavery, an increasing

25 Helen T. Catterall, *Judicial Cases Concerning American Slavery and the Negro, Carnegie Institution,* Washington, D.C., 1926, Volume I. See the Virginia cases, especially the following: *Hinde* v. *Pendleton,* Wythe 354, March 1791, 96; *Plesant* v. *Plesant,* 2 Call 319, May 1799, 105; *Henderson* v. *Allen,* 1 Hen. and M. 235, June 1807, 113; *Commonwealth* v. *Tyree,* 2 Virginia, 1821, 134; *Gregory* v. *Baugh,* 2 Lehigh 665, March 1831, 25. Several Kentucky cases were informative: *Craig* v. *McMullin,* 9 Dana 311, May 1840, 348; *Jarrett* v. *Higbee,* 5 T.B. Mon. 546, October 1827, 308; *Smith* v. *Adam,* 18 B. Mon. 685, January 1858, 432. Volume II contains cases from North Carolina, South Carolina, and Tennessee.

26 J. M. MacMaster, *A History of the People of the United States,* D. Appleton and Company, New York, 1931, Volume VIII; A. B. Hart, editor, *American History Told by Contemporaries,* The Macmillan Company, New York, 1926, Volume V; Allen Johnson, editor, *The Chronicles of America Series* (49 volumes), Yale University Press, New Haven, 1921; James Ford Rhodes, *History of the United States from the Compromise of 1850 to the Era of the Roosevelt Administration,* 9 volumes, The Macmillan Company, New York, 1929; Charles M. Andrews, *The Colonial Period of American History,* 4 volumes, Yale University Press, New Haven, 1938.

number of people opposed it on the principles of equality and justice. In proportion as the anti-slavery forces increased in the legislatures of the free states and in Congress, those tribunals evinced systems of a steady, firm and settled determination to uproot the slave system. Some of the southern anti-slavery men gathered sufficient courage to confess to themselves and to others the wrongfulness of the system.[27]

Through the medium of Congress the anti-slavery sentiment of the North was brought into active cooperation with the anti-slavery sentiment of the South. Not until northern representatives of non-slaveholding constituencies could stand on the floors of Congress, and boldly speak their minds upon the subject *and be heard,* could much be done about the abolition of slavery.

It was following that manifestation of courage that the technical legality behind which slavery entrenched itself began to be questioned, not only by the politicians, but also by churchmen and members of civic organizations. There was a growing number of people who admitted the institution of slavery had for its sanction enactments and practices of colonial times.[28] By 1861, usage as a policy was totally incapable of furnishing a satisfactory foundation for any claim of right. In this connection it is well to remember that when the colonies set forth in the Declaration of Independence the natural rights of all men to life, liberty and the pursuit of happiness, they pledged themselves to the world and to each other to recognize and maintain those rights. By 1861 many of the nation's foremost political leaders were asserting the natural-rights philosophy, strongly believing that the abolition of slavery

27 M. S. Evans, *Black and White in the Southern States,* Longmans, Green and Company, London, 1915, 46-47.

28 Irvin Wiley Bell, *Southern Negroes, 1861-1865,* Yale University Press, New Haven, 1938, 168-72.

was a debt due from the country and from the memory of the Revolutionary fathers under the principles of democracy and human nature itself.[29]

The time finally came when the ascendancy of democratic ideas was firmly established in the North and the domination of the aristocratic clique was completely put down. New organizations took form dedicated to the prevention of slavery. New political leaders grew more articulate in denouncing the system. Books began to roll off the press the purpose of which was to crystallize sentiment against slavery; liberal editorials appeared in newspapers denouncing the slave system; some ministers preached sermons against slavery while Negroes themselves sang and prayed for deliverance.[30] These efforts of the legislators, the publishers, the pulpit and the slaves took form in a new political party, the Republican.[31]

While the Republican party was in control of the national government the first and only great internal military conflict within this country took place—the Civil War. This war resulted at least in part from a consideration of the question of slavery. When one reflects upon the way slavery affected the privileged and aristocratic classes, and further upon its influence upon the concept of equality and justice, it becomes plain that the slavery question not only threatened to dissolve the Union, but required upon the battlefield the blood of several thousands of the best young men in both North and

29 Henry Wilson, *Rise and Fall of the Slave Power in America,* Houghton, Mifflin and Company, Boston, 1872, Volume III (hereafter, Wilson's *R. and F. Slave Power*).

30 The morale of the anti-slavery supporters was raised by the uncompromising denunciation of the slave system by Pope Gregory XVI in 1846. His stand, though far-reaching and important, does not form a part of the subject matter of this study.

31 The principles and platforms of this party will receive attention in Chapter III of this study.

South before it was abolished. It was a terrible fight, skill versus skill, genius versus genius, and theory versus theory. The southerners fought for local self-government and the right to enslave and govern other men; the northerners fought for universal self-government and the institution which had made such things possible without injustice to other men.

The fathers of our nation set for themselves political democracy as a goal. The people were thought of as the foundation of society. The word "people" included all of them. Thomas Jefferson had well expressed the American creed when in 1784 he said:

> Every government degenerates when trusted to the rulers of the people alone. The people themselves, therefore, are its only safe depositories . . . The influence over government must be shared among *all* the people. If every individual . . . participates of the ultimate authority, the government will be safe. . . .[32]

6. *Emancipation and Reconstruction*

In September, 1862, President Lincoln issued the Emancipation Proclamation declaring that all slaves held in the southern confederacy would be declared free on January 1, 1863, if the rebellious states had not returned to the Union by the latter date. The conditions demanded by the Proclamation were not met by the rebellious states and, as a result, the slaves were declared emancipated. In 1865, the Thirteenth Amendment of the Constitution reinforced the Emancipation Proclamation, thereby giving Lincoln's war measure the highest form of American legality.

One of the questions instantly to attract attention of the

32 *Notes on Virginia,* 1784, 207.

administration centered around protecting the freedmen in their recently attained freedom. Men in many walks of life showed a willingness to help—philanthropists, ministers, teachers and politicians. A large number of educational institutions were established and consecrated teachers struggled untiringly to raise the mental status of the former slaves.[33]

Everywhere it seems many people were in an attitude to remove the dangers and uncertainties inherent in the situation. They were not long in realizing that if the freedom which had been conferred on the former slaves were worth the price paid for it, Negroes themselves should be put in a position to protect it. It was in consequence of such a conviction that the Fourteenth Amendment was enacted, which among other things declared:

> All persons born or naturalized in the United States, and subject to the jurisdiction thereof, are citizens of the United States and of the State wherein they reside. No State shall make or enforce any law which shall abridge the privileges or immunities of citizens of the United States, nor shall any State deprive any person of life, liberty, or property without due process of law, nor deny to any person the equal protection of the law.[34]

It is hard to imagine anything needed for the protection of the freedmen not covered by this amendment. It tore asunder the dicta of Justice Taney in the Dred Scott Decision.[35] In

33 For a discussion of the education of the Negro, 1865-1900, see *Journal of Negro Education,* Howard University Press, Washington, D.C., 1943, Volume XII, Number 3; also, Henry Wilson, *R. and F. Slave Power*, 472-504.

34 Article XIV, Section I.

35 19 Howard 393.

contrast to Justice Taney's declaration that Negroes were "citizens neither of the states nor of the federal government," they were by the Fourteenth Amendment affirmed to be citizens of both.

Although the Fourteenth Amendment was thought to be airtight, flawless in its composition, and sufficient in every way to give protection to the freedmen, it was found to be legally defective. The great defect in it was in its tacit recognition of the right of a state to disfranchise the ex-slaves should it so elect. It is true that a state could not disfranchise without sacrificing some of its representation in Congress, but if it was willing to make the sacrifice, there was nothing in the amendment to prevent it.

It was to remedy such defect, so palpable and so dissonant from the concepts of the founders of our country, so contrary to the doctrine of human rights, so repugnant to the principles of Christianity, and so much in conflict with the general theories of equality of mankind, that another amendment was enacted —the Fifteenth. This amendment, furthermore, was designed to rescue the freedmen from the uncontrolled domination of the late slave-masters who were determined to prevent the freedmen from fully enjoying their newly acquired liberty.[36] It was designed, furthermore, to put into the hands of the freedmen a weapon for their own defense. The measure was strongly opposed by the Democrats of the South who used every device at their command to defeat it, while the Republicans marshaled their energy to pass it. The amendment, after several modi-

36 If one entertains any doubt about the determination of the southern former slave-masters to prevent the freedmen from enjoying the provisions of the Fourteenth and Fifteenth Amendments, he needs only to read the debates in Congress on those amendments. *Congressional Globe,* Part I, Thirty-eighth Congress, Volume XXXV, 688-94. Also, Henry Wilson's *R. and F. Slave Power,* 414-54, 647-83.

fications in both House and Senate, was carried, February 25, 1869, by the necessary two-thirds vote, and the proposed amendment was submitted to the legislatures of the states. The Fifteenth Amendment reads, Section 1:

> The right of the citizens of the United States to vote shall not be denied or abridged by the United States or by any State on account of race, color, or previous condition of servitude.

Section 2:

> The Congress shall have power to enforce this article by appropriate legislation.

The Amendment received the affirmative vote of twenty-nine states, the necessary three fourths and, on March 30, 1870, President Grant communicated the fact to Congress in a special message. Among the things the President said in his special message, two sentences are of special value in this study:

> I call the attention, therefore, of the newly enfranchised race to the importance of their striving in every honorable manner to make themselves worthy of their new privilege. To a race more favored heretofore by our laws I would say, withhold no legal privilege or advancement to the new citizens.[37]

With the help of "carpetbaggers" and "scalawags" and the United States Army, Negroes and their sympathizers were soon in control of the legislatures of several of the southern states and, at the same time, had sent several members of their race

37 Wilson, *R. and F. Slave Power,* 682.

to the national Congress and the city councils.[38] This resulted from the disfranchisement of many whites for having engaged in a war against the Union.

The story of the methods employed by the whites to reverse the situation is very well known. It involved and included intimidations by such organizations as the Pale Faces of Tennessee, the Constitutional Guard and the White Brotherhood of North Carolina, the Knights of the White Camellia in Louisiana and Arkansas, the Council of Safety in South Carolina, the Men of Justice in Alabama, the Society of the White Rose, the Seventy-six Association, and the Robinson Family in Mississippi, the Knights of the Rising Sun and the Sons of Washington in Texas.[39]

The most determined, best organized and largest of the organizations whose purpose was to circumvent the provisions of the Fifteenth Amendment was the Ku Klux Klan. It is thought to have been organized in Tennessee in 1866. Although it may have been a social organization when first organized, it soon became, at least in part, political.[40] It resorted to whippings and murder of Negroes if the ghost-like dress and gruesome voices of Klan members, usually sitting on their sheet-covered horses at night, did not prevent Negroes from going to the polls.

The Reverend A. S. Larkin, a minister of the Methodist Church, was sent by the Bishop of Ohio to northern Alabama

38 W. E. B. DuBois, *Black Reconstruction,* Harcourt, Brace and Company, New York, 1935, 404, 431-83 (hereafter, DuBois, *Black Reconstruction*).

39 Edgar T. Thompson, *Patterns of Race Conflicts,* Duke University Press, Durham, North Carolina, 1939, 138.

40 Wilson, *R. and F. Slave Power,* 630-46. The activities of that organization became so widespread that Congress appointed a Joint Committee to investigate it. After ten months, April, 1871, to February 9, 1872, the Committee issued a voluminous report in twelve volumes which covered most of the states.

to study the activities of the Ku Klux Klan. He reported that in the four years, 1868-1871, there were thirty-two murders and three hundred and forty-one whippings in that section alone.[41] It is apparent that such movements or organizations greatly deterred the Negro in his efforts to make use of the guarantees of the Fifteenth Amendment. Liberty is precious, but, without life, it is meaningless.

From 1870-77, the whites had a chance to experience the folly of committing the government into the hands of people incapable of running it efficiently due to lack of training and experience. In consequence of this lack of experience on the part of the Negro, the whites of the South became more determined not only to recapture the control of the governments, but to obtain for it legal sanction when they acquired control. The law was to be so manipulated that Negroes would be barred from future political participation. The early schemes employed are well known to students of history and consequently need no discussion here. It is necessary, however, to mention them to keep the train of events intact. There were inserted in the constitutions of the several southern states "grandfather clauses" or requirements to pay poll taxes for two years prior to election and show receipt for same, or to pass educational tests at the time the ballot was requested. These devices or requirements in no way violate the letter of the Fifteenth Amendment, but the application of those devices violated the spirit of the amendment.

It was impossible for the Negro to vote in some states because the polling judges and officials in charge of the election applied the law rigidly to Negroes but ignored the law in case of whites. Intimidation, propaganda, insertions in state constitutions of illegal provisions which were enforced against

41 *Ibid.*, 642.

Negroes by the turn of the twentieth century practically completed the disfranchisement of Negroes in the South.

The disfranchisement was aided by the rise of a new Negro leader, Booker T. Washington, who taught that the best way for the Negro to enjoy full citizenship lay in economic possession and acquiring an industrial education, not in a concerted effort to demand the ballot and manipulating political symbols.[42] Washington's philosophy was vigorously opposed by the young, brilliant W. E. B. DuBois, who insisted that the Negro should use, possess and enjoy every privilege accorded to citizens under the Constitution.[43]

Both of these men—DuBois and Washington—were soon regarded by Negroes and whites as leaders of a type. Their failure to see eye to eye on how to develop the Negro into a full-fledged American citizen tended to bewilder the Negro. In consequence of this lack of agreement, there developed three distinct schools of thought relative to the attitude and policies which should be employed by Negroes in order that their best interest be served.

First, the ultra-radical or revolutionary school. Members of this school may be characterized as having a high degree of nervous tension and by impatience with the old Negro leaders; by an insistence upon aggressive action; and by a revolt against any and every form of racial oppression. Negroes, they say, must follow the movements for economic and political betterment, such as those followed by other successful minority groups. Some of the members of this group are A. Philip Randolph, organizer of the Brotherhood of Sleeping Car Porters; Paul Robeson, the versatile artist in music and drama;

42 Booker T. Washington and W. E. B. DuBois, *The Negro in the South,* George W. Jacobs and Company, Philadelphia, 1907, 70-72.
43 DuBois, *Black Reconstruction,* 189-90.

James Ford, the Communist candidate for vice-president of the United States in 1936; and Chandler Owen, co-organizer of a radical magazine, *The Messenger.*

The editors of *The Messenger* were as much opposed to DuBois, Booker T. Washington and Moton as they were to Cole Blease, Vardaman, Heflin and Bilbo. They repudiated the Republican party and condemned the Christian church. An editorial appearing on Thanksgiving Day, 1936, declared:

> We do not thank God for anything. . . . Our Deity is the toiling masses of the world and the things for which we thank are their achievement.[44]

The thesis which the ultra-radicals attempt to support is that since Negroes as a group are unskilled, deprived of political rights and exploited in various way, they should identify themselves with organizations and movements which do not compromise with justice.[45]

Ultra-radicalism appealed to only a small number of Negroes because, first, its philosophy ran counter to the Negroes' orthodox religious traditions, and, secondly, social equality failed to function in practice as in theory. Among the things which should be mentioned as giving the ultra-radicals a tremendous appealing force are the Scottsboro Case of Alabama where nine Negro youths had been condemned to death when they had not been proved guilty, and the failure of Congress to enact

44 J. G. Van Deusen, *The Black Man in White America,* Associated Publishers, Washington, D.C., 325-26—quoting *The Messenger.*

45 *Ibid.,* 326, ex. 9, *The Forty-ninth State Movement.* A group of lawyers and outstanding citizens began a movement for a 49th state in 1933. They wrote a fundamental law, obtained a charter for their movement from the state of Illinois, and solicited citizens of their state. It had a very lofty objective—to sponsor the development of a state in the United States with a citizenry of Negroes only.

constructive legislation for the Negro. The ultra-radicals agitated unceasingly for justice in the Scottsboro Case. The agitation heightened their prestige with Negroes.

Secondly, the conservative or Booker T. Washington school. The members of this school believed in making the best of a bad situation. The Negro was taught to accept race prejudice, but to increase his economic status by industrial education and land-ownership until there was an increasing demand for him and what he developed and produced. The thesis of this group was that the Negro could acquire full-fledged citizenship more readily by economic development than by political activities.[46] This philosophy is still popular with some Negroes but has been repudiated by others. The latter group seems to be increasing. Thirdly, the liberal group. Its members urged the Negro to wage an unceasing and uncompromising fight for the enjoyment of the full rights of American citizenship as guaranteed by the Constitution. They insisted upon *identical* rights and privileges in all social and political policies and practices, and encouraged aggressive actions in an effort to attain the status of citizenship in fact as opposed to citizenship in theory.[47] The foremost leader of this school was W. E. B. DuBois, who was editor of the *Crisis* for over twenty-five years. The columns of this magazine were used to dispense his philosophy.

These facts show that shortly after the turn of this century the Negro was without any single unified leadership upon which he could rely for wholesome advice and guidance. The philosophies championed by former leaders were in conflict with each other in regard to the best techniques and methods

46 Booker T. Washington, *Up From Slavery*, Doubleday, Doran and Company, New York, 1900, 221-24.

47 W. E. B. DuBois, *The Souls of Black Folks*, The A. C. McClurg Company, Chicago, 1940, 50-52.

to be followed. Should the policy be one of active aggression or passive resistance? Should there first be insistence upon the practice of democracy and the guarantees of the Fourteenth and Fifteenth Amendments, or should the Negro first strive to prove worthy of those guarantees? Many books and articles were written shortly before and during the first decade of the twentieth century in an effort to settle the question of priority.[48] Such problems led some Negroes to seek for a solution in the courts, state and Federal. The grandfather clause was challenged and found to be without legality.[49] Success in this instance led to a belief in the United States Supreme Court as protector of Negro citizenship, and motivated Negroes to challenge other southern laws and practices.[50]

Southerners, apprehensive of the Negro's increasing numbers and intelligence, sought to accomplish their objective—isolation of Negroes from the political life of the South—by regulating membership in political parties and by the closed primary. Party qualifications were set up which were impossible for Negroes to meet. An effort was made to make the primary election a private affair, hence open only to persons whom the members of the party selected. The obvious purpose was to exclude the Negro from the Democratic Party in the primary

48 According to W. E. B. DuBois (*Black Reconstruction,* 731), the following are among the authors who believed Negroes to be subhuman and congenitally unfit for citizenship and suffrage: John W. Burgess, *Reconstruction and the Constitution, 1866-1876;* E. M. Coulter, *Civil War and Reconstruction in Kentucky;* W. W. Davis, *The Civil War and Reconstruction in Florida;* John Porter, *The Early Days of Reconstruction in South Carolina;* J. R. Ficklin, *History of Reconstruction in Louisiana.* Every writer here listed who completed a history of reconstruction in a southern state is styled an "Anti-Negro."

49 *Guinn* v. *United States,* 238 United States 347, 1915; *Newberry* v. *United States,* 256 United States 232, 1921; *Nixon* v. *Herndon,* 273 United States 536, 1927.

50 *Carrigan* v. *Buckley,* 271 United States 323, 1926; *Porter* v. *Barrett,* 233 Michigan 273, 1925.

election. If this policy was not in violation of the letter and spirit of the Constitution, the election of public officials would be a private affair, reasoned a brilliant young Texas dentist. Accordingly, he went into court in 1927, to see if the Democratic party in Texas was public or private, and, secondly, to determine whether the Texas statute of 1923 which declared "in no event shall a Negro be eligible to participate in a Democratic party primary election . . . " was not a denial of his right as a citizen.[51] The state of Texas lost the case because Texas had attempted to achieve its objective by statute. She was quick to see how the objective could be accomplished by another method.

The Texas legislature then passed another statute authorizing the state executive committee of any political party to determine who may vote in its primary. The Democratic state committee promptly passed a rule excluding Negroes from the Democratic primary of 1928. The militant Nixon, after presenting himself for membership in the Democratic party and thereafter seeking to vote in the primary, was again denied the privilege. He thereupon sued Mr. Condon, chairman of the state Democratic Committee. The case was lost in the courts of the state but was taken on appeal to the United States Supreme Court. In 1932, the Supreme Court again ruled against Texas.[52] Since 1932, the legislature has repealed its statute governing the matter. Still determined, however, the state Democratic Convention in 1932 adopted a resolution declaring that "all white citizens of the state of Texas . . . shall be eligible to membership in the Democratic party and as such entitled to participation in its deliberation.[53] In the case of

51 *Nixon* v. *Herndon,* 273 United States 536, 1927.
52 *Nixon* v. *Condon,* 280 United States 73, 1932.
53 *New York Times,* May 3, 1932, Volume II, 41.

Grovey v. Townsend,[54] the United States Supreme Court upheld the contention of Texas. The court took the position that a resolution was not the denial of any constitutional right under the Fourteenth Amendment and the exclusion thereunder did not result from a state law or the act of any state official.

Although the Negro was effectually barred from participating in the Texas primary by the dicta in Grovey v. Townsend, another case involving the Texas primary, L. E. Smith v. S. E. Allwright and J. J. Luizza was taken to the United States Supreme Court. The court rendered its decision on November 10, 1943, but since no one represented Texas, a rehearing was set for January, 1944. On April 3, 1944, the court by 8-1 ruled in favor of Dr. L. E. Smith.[55]

There have been some harmful effects of the exclusion of Negroes from political rights in the South. The policy creates a sense of injustice in his mind. Taxation without representation was as unjust from 1900 to 1940 as it was in 1776. Conferences of Negroes have constantly and repeatedly protested against the southern policy of disfranchisement. The call of the Fourth Session of the National Race Conference declared:

> The right to vote and be voted for is the first of rights. It is the vital principle of self-government and individual liberty. The ballot makes the difference between the citizen and the serf. Without the ballot the colored American is powerless to contend for right and justice and civil equality; with the ballot he is all-powerful to act in defense of every lawful privilege.[56]

54 295 United States 45, 1935.

55 *Smith* v. *Allwright,* 321 United States 649, 1944.

56 R. T. Kerlin, *The Voice of the Negro,* E. P. Dutton and Company, New York, 1920, 56.

What will be the Negro's next move falls into the realm of speculation and does not form any part of history. The challenge in the Supreme Court of many new things, such as equalization of teachers' salaries, demands for admission to the universities in the several states, and the legality of restricted residential ordinances, etc., implies that the fight for the guarantees in the Fourteenth and Fifteenth Amendments is not over.

A book of considerable size could be written in an effort to show how the Negro has proved worthy or failed to prove worthy of first-class citizenship. On the negative side of the book could be listed his illiteracy, his crime record, his poverty, his poor health and his lack of civic pride. On the positive side could be noted his achievement in the fine arts, in science, in athletics, his commercial and industrial institutions, the lengthening of his life span, his participation in the wars, his patriotism, and his response to social and civic demands.[57]

The situation confronting the Negro, that is, discrimination against him as poor and ignorant, discrimination because of color and racial origin, the "understanding" and "grandfather clauses" in constitutions of the southern states, and the "white primary," tended to keep the better class of Negroes in the South from voting after 1890; but with the shift of large numbers of Negroes from the South to the North since 1915, there has been a tendency toward toleration and liberalism in the South. Negroes, too, have shown an increasing consciousness of the value of unlimited political participation, and the better class of Negroes are now leading the way.

57 For a record of the Negro's achievements, consult the volumes of Monroe N. Work, *Negro Yearbook, 1911-1940;* and Florence Murray, *Negro Handbook, 1940-1945.* For a discussion of those who deny his proved worthiness, see the list given by W. E. B. DuBois, *Black Reconstruction,* 731.

Prior to 1915, the Negroes' thinking had very little connection with political problems. But after entering the northern industrial world, their next step was to enter into political affairs. In commenting upon the Negro in the South, W. E. B. DuBois expressed the belief that "there is not another group of twelve million people in the midst of a modern culture who has been so widely inhibited and mentally confined" as the American Negro.[58]

The South has paid a high price for its Negro disfranchisement by promoting illiteracy. White southerners in general believe that by keeping the Negro illiterate they are at the same time limiting his participation in politics. In that way the southern whites assume for themselves both the deference and the spoils. They seem not to have learned that a large number of illiterates, even though they are without political power, cannot be an asset to a democratic state. Wherever there has been a two-party system, there has been effort to woo the minority group into the fold of one of the parties. With only one political party in the South political issues become local in scope. This results in the lack of political interest on the part of most of the whites in national and often in state elections. For example, first the South was forced to accept prohibition before the adoption of the Eighteenth Amendment in order to deprive the Negro of his liquor—thus voting dry while thinking wet. Secondly, the South was exposed to such cruel characters as Tillman, Blease, Vardaman, Heflin, Talmadge and Huey Long, who, by playing on the prejudice of ignorant voters, were able to ride into office, thereby sacrificing the honor of the people of their states.

So long as the Negro remained in the South where such

58 *Black Reconstruction,* 703.

mentalities wielded the controlling influence, he had to remain politically inactive. The exodus from the South since 1915 is, therefore, of primary importance in understanding the Negro's changed political thought.

CHAPTER II

The Political Significance of the Great Migration of Negroes to the North, 1915-1940

The history of the world affords many examples of people migrating from one place to another: the movement of the Gaels, the Jutes, the Saxons and the Angles into what is now England; the Slavs, the Turks and the Arabians into south-eastern Europe; the Romans into the territory which is present-day Spain and southern France, and the Ostrogoths and Visigoths as well as many other tribes of people into those regions now called central and western Europe.[1] It is a truism that whenever people migrate, they seek something which is not readily accessible to them in their environment, or they believe that their ambitions and needs can be more easily satisfied somewhere else.

1 Warren O. Ault, *Europe in the Middle Ages,* D. C. Heath and Company, New York, 1937, 73-74. See also E. M. Hulme, *The Middle Ages,* Henry Holt and Company, New York, 1929, Chapters II, III, and IV.

62365

The migration of Negroes in large numbers from the southern parts of the United States to the North, taking on accelerated speed in 1915, follows the general pattern of other migrating and immigrating people in other parts of the world both in remote and in recent years. Many of the migrating Negroes had been led to believe that the things which were difficult, if not impossible, for them to attain in the South could be acquired in the North with little or no effort.[2] Such thoughts spread to his actions in the political as well as the economic sphere; hence, the Negro's migration cannot be accounted for on any single basis. There were many motives for the Negro's migration, ranging all the way from disrupted love affairs to the hope of satisfying political ambitions. We are here concerned with the effects which the migration of large numbers had on their political behavior. Just how their migration to the North affected their political thought and political behavior is a worthy investigation, especially so since Negroes constitute about 10 per cent of the population, and since in America we boast of our democratic institutions and practices. Our interest here is further circumscribed by its potential and its actual significance.

It has been ably asserted that the economic motive caused a greater number to migrate than any other single motive. There are indeed those who believe that if the economic motives were not the only ones, they were the primary ones.[3]

2 *Chicago Defender,* Chicago Defender Publishing Company, Chicago, issues of June 10, 1916; Oct. 9, 1920; April 1, 1922.

3 T. Arnold Hill, *The Negro and Economic Reconstruction,* Associates in Negro Education, Washington, D.C., 1937, 27-28. S. D. Spero and A. L. Harris, *The Black Worker,* Columbia University Press, New York, 1931, 385-388. Arna Bontemps and Jack Conroy, *They Seek a City,* Doubleday, Doran and Company, New York, 1945, Introduction, xi. Kingsley Morris, "The Negro Comes North," *Forum,* Forum Publishing Company, New York, 1922, 181-90.

Central Bible College Library
Springfield, Missouri

To argue motives would achieve little in this undertaking, for whatever it was, the undeniable fact is that the Negro population in the northern states was greatly increased during the period 1915-1940; and their potential strength was rapidly politically harnessed.

Indeed, the *Literary Digest* declared, "The Black Belt is growing broader in northern cities—in New York, Chicago, Philadelphia, Detroit, and Pittsburgh." After that declaration, the editor asked the meaning of those population shifts and brought to bear excerpts from a number of newspapers in an effort to give political meaning to those shifts. Quoting from the Asheville, North Carolina *Citizen,* he said, "The population shifts are of the greatest potential importance," and then followed certain valuable statistics in support of his contention, thus:

> Out of a total Negro population of 11,891,143, the census shows that 9,361,577 are still in the South, an increase for the decade of 5 per cent; while 2,409,219 are in the North, an increase for the decade of 63.6 per cent. The West now has 120,347 Negroes, or 531 per cent more than in 1920. During the ten-year period 1920-1930, the Negro population of the West and North increased by 978,666, as compared with the increase in the South of 449,346.[4]

After having shown what the increases were in the Negro population in the North and West, he enumerated the increases by saying, "At least three quarters of a million Negroes migrated from the South during this decade, 1920-1930."

During that decade three southern states—Georgia, South

4 George F. Havell, *Literary Digest*, New York, Volume CX, August 29, 1931, 4.

Carolina and Virginia—showed losses in Negro population while several northern states showed increases in Negro population —for example, Michigan, 182 per cent; New York, 108 per cent; Illinois, 80 per cent; New Jersey, 78 per cent; Ohio, 66.1 per cent; and Pennsylvania, 51.5 per cent.[5]

Warning should be given here of the limitations of intellectual analysis as a way of truth. In any attempt to explain causal relations one cannot proceed without positing certain values as being more significant than others. Causation can be explained only by selecting certain factors as being more meaningful than others. The consequences of this logical dilemma are graphically shown in a familiar anecdote: A student who has just had three or four cocktails is shaving when his roommate slams the door. He drops the razor and cuts his toe; he then carelessly ties up the wound and goes to the theater. His toe becomes inflamed, and he finally dies. What is the cause of his death? The following causes, among others, may be assigned by various persons: General septicemia, by the doctor; a streptococcus infection, by the bacteriologist; no one to take proper care of him, by his mother; lack of discipline in the boy's upbringing, by the uncle; the boy's neglect of the wound, by a timid, methodical friend; the cocktails, by a prohibitionist.

Thus it is with any logical analysis of the great migration of Negroes to the North, 1915-1940. One can discover some of the causes of some of the Negroes' migration from some places, but there was no one cause which covers all of the cases. The emphasis which one places upon any given motive may depend upon the person discussing the migration.

Even though the great bulk of Negroes were still in the South, the facts stated above represent far-reaching changes, for

5 *Fifteenth Census of the United States, 1930,* Volume VII, "Population," Government Printing Office, Washington, D.C., 37.

they show that almost two thirds of the entire increase in the Negro population in the decade 1920-1930 occurred in the North.

A very scholarly study shows that in the single year ending September 1, 1923, more than 478,700 Negroes migrated from thirteen southern states for the North and West. Commissioner Phil H. Brown of the Department of Labor reached that conclusion by utilizing data supplied to him by state, municipal and civic statisticians and officials. He worked out a table which indicated the colored population of each of the thirteen southern states, the number of colored migrants, the proportion that those formed to the colored population and the proportion that each state furnished to the total migration for that year.[6] Although the number of Negroes who left the South cannot be established with certainty, since no official record was made, we are able to get a fairly authentic notion of the increase by comparing the numbers in certain northern cities in 1910 and 1920. In an article in *Current History Magazine* by E. D. Walrond, there is given an account of those increases in thirty-three strategic cities in the North. He found that the percentage increased from a low of 11.9 in Denver, Colorado, to a high of 786.5 in Akron, Ohio. In two cities, the Negro population increased over 200 per cent—Toledo and Youngstown, Ohio; one had an increase of 307 per cent—Cleveland, Ohio; and one had an increase of 623.4 per cent—Detroit, Michigan.[7] In an article in the *New Republic,* July 18, 1923, under the title of "The Negro Comes North," Mr. Walrond lists many of the reasons for the Negro's northward migration. His language will admit of improvement in neither clarity nor coherence.

6 *Monthly Labor Review,* United States Department of Labor Statistics, Volume XVIII, 1924, 762-63, Government Printing Office, Washington, D.C., (hereafter referred to as *Labor Review).* See also *World Almanac,* New York World Publishing Company, New York, 1924, 386-87.

7 New York Times Company, New York, Volume XVIII, 1924, 942-43.

> Statistics show that in four months the increase in Negro migration jumped from 850—the normal influx—to 12,000 in a single month (1923). The Chicago stockyards advertised for 50,000 Negro laborers. Chartering the Illinois Central for transportation, the Negro dropped hoe and shovel, hastily answered the call. That event marked the real beginning of the 1916-1918 migration. It swept from Chicago to Detroit, the colored population of which city was increased over four hundred per cent . . . For weeks the *Chicago Defender,* a Negro weekly, carried across the top of its front page in bold-face type the magic sign, "Come up North. Why Stay down South."[8]

A careful analysis of the quotation above will show it to be neither correct in all details nor general in application, but a more correct and a more generally accepted description of what was taking place has not been made.

There were two waves or periods of accelerated migration: the first, 1916-1918, when over 450,000 Negroes went North; the other in 1923, when as indicated above, over 478,700 went North in that single year. After 1919 there was a sharp decline, and the migration did not revive until 1922. There was also a period of stagnation in Negro migration to the North in 1924.[9] The periods of stagnation in migration do not mean that there was no migration, but that it was not as conspicuous as it was in some other periods. The "pull" of the North—the land of opportunity where financial, educational, social, and political status could be obtained—contrasted with the "push" of the

8 New Republic Publishing Co., New York, Volume XXXV, 1923, 200-1. Also Abram L. Harris, "Negro Migration to the North," *Current History Magazine*, Volume XX, 1924, 924-25.

9 *Labor Review*, Volume XVIII, 943.

South—with its pattern of segregation, social ostracism, poor pay, and the absence of educational opportunities or the lack of justice in the courts, led an increasing number of Negroes to change their places of residence as well as their minds.

Careful study of the table which Commissioner Brown worked out shows most conclusively that the states in which racial intolerance and mob violence occurred most frequently were the states from which the highest percentage of Negroes migrated 1921-1923: Alabama, 18.8 per cent; Georgia, 25.2 per cent; Florida, 18.8 per cent; and Mississippi, 17.3 per cent.[10] Those four states contributed 79.1 per cent of the Negro migration to the North in 1923 and in the two years 1921-1922, there were more Negroes lynched in those four states than in the other nine southern states combined.[11]

In the light of those facts, what a prominent Negro physician gives as his reason for leaving the state of Mississippi becomes increasingly significant:

> I left the South not in an effort to make more money than I was making in Meridian, Mississippi, but I left in order that my children might have an opportunity to develop their talents and capacities unhampered and unrestrained by a prejudiced and personality-dwarfing environment. Observation and experience had taught me that the average southern Negro was possessed with an inferiority complex that he would not have had, had he been in a northern environment. For a Negro child to be reared in the South in his early and formative years is to take the chance of stifling his mentality

10 *Monthly Labor Review,* Volume XVIII, 762.

11 "The Lawless Nation," editorial in *The Nation,* Volume CXXIX, Number 3344, August 7, 1929, 134. See also *Chicago Bee,* Chicago Bee Publishing Company, Chicago, July 4 and 11, 1928.

> and curbing his ambitions. The way to avoid those possibilities was for me to take them away to a place where the doors of opportunity were open to them or at least not tightly shut simply because they are Negroes.[12]

More light was thrown on the various causes for migration by analyzing the replies received to a questionnaire sent to 110 persons, all of whom migrated from the South between 1915-1925. Seventy-eight were filled out and returned. Analysis shows that the motive for migration depended largely upon the economic and social status of the migrating persons. Of twenty-one who claimed that they migrated for reasons other than economic, that is, cultural, social, educational or political, nine were lawyers; seven, physicians; two, dentists; one, teacher; one, minister; and one who gave no occupation or profession. On the other hand, of the fifty-seven who did not list social, cultural or political reasons for their migration, but economic, six were barbers; four, waiters; five, butchers; four, Pullman porters; three, auto mechanics; three, tailors; and thirty-nine listed themselves as common laborers.[13] The number of replies might be too small upon which to base any far-reaching conclusion that has bearing upon a general thesis, yet they were sufficient in variety and scope to indicate that the Negro elite was actuated in its migration by consideration not prevalent among the rank and file of Negroes. To state the conclusion differently, the motive for the migration of Negroes from the South depended upon who they were, economically and culturally—the "upper crust" or the "lower crust" in the Negro hierarchy.

12 Letter from Dr. E. E. Howard, August 21, 1945. Incidentally, Dr. Howard is the son of a former member of the Mississippi legislature, and the brother of Perry W. Howard, who has been the National Republican Committeeman from Mississippi for the past twenty-five years. See Appendix 2.

13 For the type of questions asked, see Appendix 1.

Proved by both psychology and experience, it is no longer a question for debate that a very small number of people do the thinking and shaping of behavior patterns of the masses. The Negro is no exception. A casual observation of his political activities in a few northern cities—Chicago, Cleveland, New York, Kansas City, Detroit, Philadelphia and Cincinnati—illustrates the point.[14] There were a few so-called "upper crust"[15] Negroes who assumed the leadership of the group in the North when political choices and decisions had to be made.[16] There are many examples of abuse of such confidence by the Negro leaders and of proven unworthiness;[17] but because there were not better leaders known who would assume this responsibility—civic and political—the Negroes in these cities acquiesced to the suggestions and dictates of such persons.

The question might be asked: Where were the Negroes going and what percentage of skilled workers were included in the number? In 1924, an effort was made to answer that question scientifically. In order to arrive at a conclusion pay-roll data were secured from 276 employers of Negro labor in the states of California, Connecticut, Delaware, Illinois, Indiana, Kansas, Kentucky, Maryland, Massachusetts, Michigan, Missouri, New Jersey, New York, Ohio and Oklahoma. At the time of the study, April 30, 1923, there were 60,421 Negroes employed in those states; of that number 19,474 were interviewed. The num-

14 *Literary Digest,* Volume CX, August 29, 1931, 4.

15 The term "upper-crust Negro" is not restricted to those of education and wealth but, as here used, it applies to those whose wisdom and integrity, although known at times to be questionable by the recently migrated Negroes, was accepted, nevertheless, as their criteria for action.

16 Harold F. Gosnell, *Negro Politicians,* University of Chicago Press, Chicago, 1935, Chapter IV.

17 A very excellent treatment of this point is given by Lewis A. H. Caldwell, "The Policy Game in Chicago," Master's thesis, Northwestern University, Evanston, Illinois, August, 1937, 47-58.

ber which had gone directly North and West from the South and had obtained employment that year was 4,702 or 23 per cent of those interviewed.[18] It is revealing to note that the number of skilled laborers who migrated from the South to the North was considerably smaller than the number of unskilled. According to Commissioner Phil H. Brown, it was less than 5 per cent.[19] That situation was due, at least in part, to the fact that skilled labor in the North was organized, while in the South it was not; and also to the fact that most of the skilled labor—carpentry, bricklaying, barbering, mechanical work, tailoring, and blacksmithing—in the South was done by Negroes, but in the North the unions generally refused to admit Negroes as members.

A large number of the Negroes who went North left southern rural communities, that is, they first left the rural areas of the South for the urban communities of the South. Then, before becoming adjusted to southern urban life, they left those communities for the northern cities.[20] This put a southern rural Negro into a northern urban community. It is not a surprise, then, to find that they were socially and economically maladjusted.

That fact has a double significance because it affects both the North and the South in their political and economic policies.

1. The Effect Upon the South of the Negro Migration

In the South the effect was felt first in the economic sphere. There was a shortage of servants in the homes, a shortage of

18 *Labor Review,* Volume XVIII, 66.

19 *Ibid.,* 62.

20 *Negro Migration, 1916-1917,* United States Department of Labor, 1919, 19-31. Also, *Negroes in the United States, 1920-1932,* United States Bureau of the Census, 1935, 21-35. A discussion of the rural-urban movement is given in detail (page 00 below) where it fits more properly into the context.

laborers in the factories, a shortage of farm hands, and a labor shortage on the railroads.[21] The effect showed itself again when the whites in an effort to alter the situation greatly increased wages and, to an extent, changed the traditional relationship from that of lord and serf to one of employer and employee. Even southern organized labor showed signs of tolerance in that certain specialized or skilled Negro workers were admitted to membership.[22] In the urban communities to which Negroes migrated from the rural areas, the southern city officials began to improve the sanitary conditions of the sections in which Negroes lived, and in some instances health leagues were organized among them.[23]

There are several examples in which the Chambers of Commerce in different southern cities invited prominent Negroes to attend their meetings from time to time to suggest remedies for the Negroes' grievances in the South and to help to check the migration. What was said by one Negro at such a meeting in Birmingham, Alabama, is inspirational and thought-provoking. After he stated what the grievances were, and after suggesting remedies, he declared that the Negroes had become conscious that they were badly treated in the South and that their only alternative seemed to have been for them to leave.

> You will not reform and they cannot conform. Since that is the situation, they are using that method [migration] of avoiding the unpleasant and undemocratic practices which you people follow down here.[24]

21 Emmett J. Scott, *Negro Migration During the World War,* Carnegie Endowment for International Peace (Economic Studies of the War, Number 16), Washington, D.C. (hereafter referred to as Scott's *Negro Migration*).

22 *Ibid.,* 92.

23 *Ibid.,* 98-99.

24 *Opportunity, Journal of Negro Life,* Official Organ of the National Urban League, National Urban League, New York, Volume III, 1923.

A little later in the meeting, he pointed out that it was impossible to bring back from the North those who had gone there and were making good, and suggested that the meeting could more wisely utilize its time and effort by formulating policies which would hold those who had not gone. During the entire address the audience gave him full attention, and he concluded by suggesting that after policies were formulated they would have to be enforced. He suggested a very simple policy—that the whites must change their attitude toward the Negroes first, and their treatment, second.

In some places, it seems that an earnest effort was made by a few whites to check the Negro exodus by putting those suggestions into practice. There were several new schools built in some states; farmers who had been in debt all their lives not only "paid out" but "cleared" money. White men were seen standing on the streets and in the roads talking freely with Negro men (a thing unusual and very rarely done then), and some Negro and white ministers exchanged pulpits on a few Sundays in a few places.[25]

25 Reverend Ross D. Brown tells the following story, which he declares to be true, about a Negro man who accompanied his minister to a white church where the colored minister was to preach one Sunday. After the sermon an opportunity was given to those who wished to join the church by the assistant pastor (white). The Negro got up instantly at the invitation and presented himself for membership in that church. The assistant pastor thereupon questioned him about his conversion, his reasons for wanting to join that church, if he could not be of greater service to God and man were he to affiliate himself with a colored church, etc. Finally he suggested to the colored man that he should go home and earnestly pray over the matter, asking God to direct him in the situation. The colored man is said to have taken the assistant minister's suggestion; he went home and prayed over the matter for a week, and on the following Sunday morning returned to the same church, prepared to give his answer. When the assistant pastor asked, "John, have you asked the Lord about the matter? What did He say?" To the surprise of the audience, John, the colored man, answered that he had prayed over the matter and God had given

The Negroes as a group feel that most of the southern whites are hypocritical, which hypocrisy carries over into their every act and permeates their entire being; hence they say the whites of the South are not to be trusted when they speak about the Negro question, for they have too often used Esau's hand and Jacob's voice.[26] The Negro, apprehensive toward the favorable consideration shown him in the South, questioned the permanence of such treatment and wondered whether or not after the emergency was over a greater intolerance would result than had yet been known.[27] Therefore, in spite of efforts to prevent their northward migration, they (Negroes) continued to leave the South in ever-increased numbers.[28] This situation led some of the southern states to attempt to regulate migration by enacting laws under the provisions of which out-of-state agents were required to pay fees in order to operate within their borders. Those fees were sufficiently high in places to become prohibitive to those agents–ranging from $1,000 in South Carolina to $5,000 in Mississippi.[29] When the Negroes became aware of those laws, they ceased to gather in cities to meet agents, not only out of consideration of their own safety, but also for the safety of the agents as well. On many occasions both were threatened. Agents

an answer to his prayers. The assistant pastor nervously repeated the question, "What did the Lord say?" The colored man replied, "The Lord said to me that if I could get into this church, I could do more than He could," and walked out. Reverend Brown is author of two works popular among Negroes, *Watch My Race Go By* and *The Afro-American Almanac.* He is a forceful speaker and for that reason is in constant demand to fill pulpits and lecture halls. The incident above, he declared, was one which occurred near Brookhaven, Mississippi, in July, 1918.

26 Robert R. Morton, *What the Negro Thinks,* Doubleday, Doran and Company, New York, 1932, 134.

27 Scott, *Negro Migration,* 101-3.

28 *Negroes in the United States, 1920-1932; 1932-1940,* United States Department of Commerce, Bureau of the Census, Government Printing Office, Washington, D.C., 1941, 12.

29 *Ibid.,* 925.

were smuggled into some communities, however, or Negroes would meet them in some inconspicuous place and arrange for transportation.[30] Just how they knew when the "agent" or "pass rider" was coming was a secret that only a few shared. Nevertheless, the "agent" usually secured a substantial number upon his "visits." There were several instances in which the agents were apprehended and were required to pay heavy fines or face jail sentences, but those instances served to advertise to the Negro the opportunities in the North. In most of the trials the agent was represented by northern lawyers who at times denounced in bitter terms many of the conditions in the South, and Negroes either read what had been said in the papers, heard it in court, or heard it in the houses of the whites where some of them were employed.[31]

2. *The Effects Upon the North of the Negro Migration*

There were two basic circumstances which made the Negro look to the North in his political aspirations. First, national power was more concentrated there, for the South then, as now, was quite like a minority group itself—a kind of a problem to the nation and to itself; and secondly, the Negroes had the ballot in the North. Those two circumstances served to remove from the thinking of the politically aspiring Negro every prop employed by the southerners to prevent him from going North. The first migration of the Negro was not from the South to the North, as was said above, but from the rural areas to the urban areas. Since 1910 Negroes have moved into urban areas in the South as well as into the industrial North. In 1910, 2,684,797 Negroes, or about 27 per cent, lived in towns and cities (that is, centers of population of 2,500 or over); in 1930, 5,193,913, or

30 *Ibid.*, 925.
31 Scott, *Negro Migration*, 35-39.

about 43 per cent lived in towns and cities. That urbanization was in accordance with the general trend of the whole population in the United States. The town and city dwellers for all classes represented 46 per cent of the population in 1910, and 56 per cent in 1930. Thus Negro migration to cities was much swifter during the period 1910-1930, although the Negro was still below the average urbanization of the nation.[32] A few more statistics here will lend themselves to clarity. In 1910, the Negroes constituted 1.8 per cent of the population of the North; in 1920, 2.3 per cent; in 1940, 3.6 per cent.[33] The Negro population in the North in the decade 1930-1940 increased 15.8 per cent; while in the South it increased 5.8 per cent; and in the West, 41.8 per cent.[34] There is only one interpretation which can be made from those facts, and that is that the efforts of the South to deter northward Negro migration had been futile. In fact, nearly every southern urban community showed a decrease in its Negro population during that decade similar to the one of the decade 1920-1930, while the proportion in northern cities was increased.[35]

How was their political thought and behavior affected by residence in northern cities? It is a fact recognized from the time of Plato that political behavior is more pronounced and articulate in cities than in rural areas or thinly populated regions. That has been especially true in the United States when the two major political parties have been doubtful about the

32 *Negro Migration in 1916-1917,* United States Department of Labor, 1919, 1. Also, *Negroes in the United States 1920-1932,* United States Bureau of the Census, 1935, 28-47.

33 *Negroes in the United States, 1920-1932; 1932-1940,* United States Department of Commerce, Bureau of the Census, Government Printing Office, Washington, D.C., 12. See also Florence Murray, editor, *The Negro Handbook,* A. A. Wyn, Inc., New York, 1944, 15.

34 Murray, *op. cit.,* 15.

35 Monroe N. Work, *The Negro Yearbook,* Tuskegee Institute, Tuskegee, Alabama, 1937, 255. Also, Murray, *op. cit.,* 17.

support they would receive from large groups or interests when it appeared that the contest would be close. When the Negroes penetrated the North in large numbers, not only did their presence create the possibility of tightening the election, but one must remember that the Democratic party was stronger in many of the industrial cities in the North than the Republican party was in the southern cities. In addition to this the Negro seems to have been alert in realizing that his political interest should be local at first, that only after gaining the experience to cope with local situations should he interest himself in state and national political affairs. For these reasons, many young men who had attended northern schools, both colleges and universities, when they settled in the northern industrial cities to begin their careers, became active in local politics. They aligned themselves with the party in power and became articulate in declaring their best interest could be served by helping to determine "who gets what" in the city, not "who gets what" in the state capital or in the nation's capital.[36] Accordingly in New York City and Boston, both Democratic strongholds, Negroes became active with the local Democratic machines as early as 1917.[37]

In 1925, during the mayoralty campaign of J. J. Walker, the Democratic candidate, that eccentric young man in a speech in Harlem, the area in New York which is largely dominated by Negroes, declared, "I won't do a thing for Negroes. Nor will I do anything for Jews or Irishmen. But as mayor of this great city, I will work for the people."[38] Negroes in Harlem regarded that stand as an expression of an equalitarian principle which

36 Harold F. Gosnell, *Negro Politicians*, University of Chicago Press, Chicago, 1935. Introductory chapter by R. E. Parks.

37 Claude McKay, *Harlem: Negro Metropolis*, E. P. Dutton and Co., New York, 1940, 121 ff. (hereafter referred to as Claude McKay).

38 *New York Times*, October 8, 1925. Also November 1, 1925.

Negro leaders seemed proud to hear. As a consequence of that speech, along with other considerations shown them, a large number of Negroes went Democratic and have remained Democrats ever since.[39] The Democrats gave the Negro good returns for supporting them, not sugar-coated pills in the form of praise for their past loyalties and promises which were never kept, but jobs and consideration.[40] That was not an entirely new policy, for as early as 1919 Ferdinand Q. Morton was appointed Assistant District Attorney through "boss" Charles F. Murphy, who had championed the Negro cause in Tammany Hall. The Democrats continued their policy and, by 1936, there were several Negroes holding positions of honor and distinction in New York City. For example, there were one district leader for Tammany Hall, two municipal judges, two aldermen, two assemblymen, one assistant state attorney, three assistant district attorneys, one member of the city Civil Service Commission, and a large number of clerks, deputy sheriffs, secretaries, policemen and teachers.[41] The pay roll for Negroes in New York City in that year, including teachers, exceeded $3,000,000, most of which came by way of Tammany Hall.[42]

The question now might be broached: What bearing did the migration have upon the political significance of the Negro? An editorial in the *Cincinnati Post,* June 15, 1917, gives an excellent answer to such a query. After the editor had given a description of the congested living quarters of the Negroes in that city, which he said could be duplicated in many other cities, he declared that in one ward there were 2,793 Negroes registered

39 Claude McKay, 126.

40 *New Republic,* Volume XXXV, 200-201.

41 *54th Anual Report of Municipal Civil Service Commissioner,* Paul R. Kern, President, New York, 1937, 43-44. More will be said about achievements of the Negro in Chapter V, "The Negro and the Democratic Party."

42 Claude McKay, 122.

whose ages were between 21 and 31 and that that number exceeded the next most thickly populated non-Negro ward by over 600. He continued by saying "those men will be voted in bloc and thereby determine who the mayor, the judges, and other officials of this city will be."[43]

It was the congestion or concentration of the Negroes that gave the northern politicians most concern, for it made them, the Negroes, a threat to any political party that they opposed, if not in the congressional district or the city, at least in the ward where they lived. To grasp fully the significance and implications of this fact, one should be cognizant that the states are divided into congressional districts, countries, cities, wards and precincts for administrative and political purposes. When a large number of people are concentrated into any of these areas they may by their union with what was formerly a weak party win elections in such regions. It was imperative therefore for both parties to initiate programs which would appeal to the Negro in an effort to conserve his support or obtain it. Republicans felt that they "carried the Negro around in their vest pocket," according to the expression of Senator Mark Hanna, while the Democrats knew that if they were to get the Negro votes they had to break down the Negro's loyalty to the Republican party. Democrats worked while Republicans slept as far as the Negro was concerned.

The Democrats' work was the more effective because of the characteristics noticeable among newly arrived Negroes in the North. Negroes were comparatively innocent in politics; they knew nothing about strategy or political bargaining; hence, it was inevitable for them to fall prey to the "machine" and the "ring." Seeing his innocence, the "boss," working with the politicians of the underworld, began to exploit the Negro not

43 *Cincinnati Post*, June 15, 1917.

only out of his money in the policy and numbers racket, but also out of his votes.[44]

The exploitation of the Negro took several forms: sometimes Negroes were paid to vote for a given candidate; sometimes the ballot boxes in the precincts where the Negroes lived in great numbers were stuffed; sometimes certain speakers were employed to *misinform* Negroes relative to marking their ballots so as to make them "scratch" the ballot; sometimes Negroes were told that a vote for a certain person meant Negroes would be returned to the South and to slavery, or that the political "boss" would take away the jobs which Negroes held if Negroes supported designated parties or persons.[45]

These were not the worst forms of exploiting the politically innocent Negroes in the North. When certain politicans realized how Negroes in ever-increasing numbers were becoming conscious of the value of the ballot and the likelihood of its use presently for the nomination and election of members of their own race, some local white office-holders in certain regions were alarmed.[46] Accordingly these local white politicians devised schemes to perpetuate themselves in office. By obtaining aid of their friends who were public office-holders, local and state laws were enacted to change the boundaries of the ward or congressional district so as to divide the voting strength of the Negroes.[47]

44 Lewis A. H. Caldwell, *The Policy Game in Chicago,* 47-48. Mr. Caldwell gives an interesting account of the methods and techniques employed to exploit the Negroes out of their money in those games, but the general body of that information, though important, has no place in this study; only the disclosure that those men who financed the policy game were also the heaviest contributors to the campaign funds of both parties in local elections is relevant. See also H. F. Gosnell, *Negro Politicians*, University of Chicago Press, Chicago, 1935, Chapter IV.

45 *Chicago Defender*, November 4 and 11, 1924.

46 H. F. Gosnell, *Negro Politicians,* 1-20.

47 *Chicago Bee,* October 3, 1928.

In some places local politicians seemed to have shared Hitler's philosophy in part at least: "Divide and destroy." The device they used is called gerrymandering; since 1926 it has been employed in Chicago, Cleveland, Detroit, New York, Kansas City, Pittsburgh, St. Louis and Philadelphia. Each time it divided the regions where Negroes were most thickly concentrated so as to prevent other Negroes from receiving additional positions by election to public offices.[48]

An editorial in *The Chicago Bee,* a Negro weekly, might be instructive and informative here. It declared:

> Outside of their prescribed districts, it seems impossible to elect Negroes to public political office. Time was in Chicago and Cook County when colored representatives were elected to the county board and the municipal court bench, positions requiring the candidate to poll a large majority of city-wide votes for election which they did. In recent years candidates for those elective offices have been defeated. In the mixed fourth ward some years ago there was the possibility of electing a colored alderman, the great bigwig colored politicians said, no, the time isn't ripe yet. The same argument was used when Congressman Martin B. Madden was overdue to be replaced by a colored congressman. When the time was ripe to elect a colored alderman from the fourth ward the politicians changed the boundary line with the connivance of Negro politicians, so another elective office was lost to us.[49]

It is an obvious fact that those newly arrived Negroes from the South would be Republican in their politics if they had been

48 *Municipal Reference Library Notes,* New York Public Library, New York, 1927, 6-9.

49 Chicago Bee Publishing Company, Chicago, February 2, 1936.

left alone. The fact is that they were not left alone, for the Democrats readily saw their potential power in a so-called democracy. They, therefore, assumed it as their first responsibility to woo the Negroes from the Republican party. That, the Democrats knew, could best be done by making political concessions by putting members of the Negro race in positions of high trust carrying great deference, power and big pay. In New York, the Democrats discovered as early as 1922 that the Negroes were not believing in the divinity of the Republican party when the Negroes of Harlem sent a member of the Democratic party to represent the twenty-first district to Albany.[50]

In 1924, there was more evidence that the Democrats were wooing the Negroes from the Republican party when they elected Henry W. Shields, a Negro, to the state legislature on the Democratic ticket.[51] In 1924, the acid test was applied to the Negro's Republican loyalty in New York City. In that year the Democratic organization placed the names of two colored lawyers on their ticket as candidates for the bench in the city courts; the Republican organization did likewise. A study of the returns indicates that the votes for the four Negroes in districts outside Harlem were very close indeed, but in the Harlem precints and wards the Democratic candidates received a large plurality and were elected.[52]

The Democrats broke into the Republicans' ranks with the Negroes, not only in New York but also in other northern cities. One example will suffice to illustrate the point. In Cleveland, Ohio, in 1926, a Negro man in describing what had taken place there in the political arena to the National

50 *New York Age* (a Negro weekly), New York Age Publishing Company, New York, November 20, 1922.

51 *Amsterdam News* (a Negro weekly), Amsterdam News Company, New York, November 16, 1922.

52 *Ibid.*

Association for the Advancement of Colored People, declared:

> At the state election in 1926, we supported Democrats and the Republicans alike, depending upon their merits, and helped to achieve the defeat of the Republican candidate for governor and lieutenant governor and helped to elect a Democratic sheriff in this county.[53]

The following year the Negroes again demonstrated independence of party labels when they placed in the field three Negro candidates for public office: Mr. Fleming, a Republican who was returned to the city hall for the eighth time; Dr. E. J. Gregg, with the endorsement of the Democratic organization, who was elected from the same district along with Mr. Fleming; and Claybourne George, who was elected from the fourth district as an independent in politics.[54] Those nominations and campaigns which resulted in the election of Republicans, Democrats and Independents doubtless made the politicians in Cleveland aware of the fact that the Negro's vote was a prize worthy of effort, for it was then wedded to no particular party label as was justifiably assumed formerly.

It can be said in summary that the migration of Negroes from the South to the North after 1915 required of the Negroes to make a series of adjustments. They had not developed as a group the techniques and skills with which to manipulate effectively the political symbols; but because of their concentration in northern industrial centers their political potentialities were readily seen, which potentialities gave them tremendous significance. The Democratic party, because it knew that the Negroes were traditionally Republicans, began to seek the Negroes' support in several large cities, while the Republican

53 *Cleveland Plain Dealer*, November 11, 1926. See also *Cleveland News*, November 11, 1926.

54 *Cleveland News, ibid.*

party felt as Mark Hanna said, "I carry the Negro's vote around in my vest pocket," and was consequently indifferent.

The Democratic party of the North was generous in that it not only gave the Negroes training in practical politics by permitting them to participate in nominating and electing candidates, but also by permitting them to serve as judges at the polling places and in many other ways. It would be a grave mistake for one to assume that the Negroes prior to this time had no political experience.

A study of the history of the Reconstruction period would show the contrary to be true. The Negroes began to use that newly acquired training to nominate and elect members of their race to public office, first to the city halls and later to the state's capitals. They were confronted by a variety of problems put in their way by white officeholders who were determined to perpetuate their own political existence. The most prominent device used by the whites was the gerrymander. The Republicans shared in the use of those devices as well as the Democrats; however, the evidence tends to indicate that the gerrymander was initiated by the Republicans, for it was they who felt that they had a monopoly on the Negro's loyalty and support. When the Republicans found that such was no longer true it seems that they were all the more determined to reduce the Negro to a nonentity in politics. It was not until the Democrats had wooed large number of Negroes into their fold in many cities that the Republicans realized that Negroes were thinking beings, thinking of political as well as other advantages. That situation ushered in a contest between the two major parties, the purpose of which was to gain and keep the Negro's support. That contest was most articulate in the presidential campaigns of 1936 and 1940.

Thus the migration to the North by a large number of

Negroes from the South had a dual effect: an effect upon the South in that it showed the South how dependent it was on the Negro economically, and, as a consequence, the spirit of tolerance was temporarily awakened; an effect upon the North in that it put into its midst a new factor to be reckoned with in running a democratic state—the Negro. The city or state "boss" and the political "machines" along with the politicians and racketeers, all exploited the innocent Negro. That exploitation, although not as articulate now as it has been at certain periods in the past, was carried forward under the WPA and other New Deal agencies, 1936-1940.

Although no minority is able to protect itself against any powerful organization such as the city "boss" and the political "machines," constant exposure to them will make one search for means of protection. The Negroes did just that in many instances, for example, the protest movements, such as the March on Washington, the lobbyists, the National Association for the Advancement of Colored People, and similar movements. One sees that in 1915 at the beginning of the great migration from the South to the North, the Negro in the North thought very little about political activities; but in 1940, if one judges the Negro's political thought by the amount of space devoted to it in the Negro newspapers and magazines, politics was uppermost. The Negro's interests in political affairs since his new achievements in politics ramify in all directions and touch everything from the precinct in which he lives to the great international congresses and conferences at Teheran, Yalta, San Francisco and Potsdam.

CHAPTER III

The Negro and the Republican Party, 1865-1932

The founders of the Republican party were motivated in their endeavors by at least three considerations: first, they opposed local sovereignty, which John C. Calhoun had ably defended until his death in 1850; secondly, they wanted to control the entire nation; thirdly, they denied that a state had a right to secede from the Union. The things for which the party was contending and the program it assigned to itself involved an interpretation and construtíon of the Constitution. These were to have far-reaching effects on many of the economic, social and political issues with which the nation would be confronted in the immediate future. Among the questions raised by its position and program were: Could the slavery issue be dodged? Was the Union an end in itself? How should the government respond to the growing forces in the North and West, etc.? It was from such issues and problems that the Civil War arose. Later, many matters which had been in the hands of the states were taken away from them and controlled by the Federal government. One of those matters was human slavery, which the Federal government abolished by the Thirteenth Amendment which followed the war measure known as the Emancipation Proclamation.

A series of reforms followed the Civil War, some of which strengthened the Republican party in the thinking of the Negro. Frederick Douglass, one of the most influential Negro leaders, in that period declared that he was convinced that the Republican party was the Negroes' friend and merited their support and loyalty.[1] In confirmation of such a belief, some who were influential in the party's council expressed a sense of responsibility for carrying out the pledges and policies of the Republican party.[2]

Winning the war and abolishing slavery were not all to which the Republican party had pledged itself for the uplift of Negroes when it was organized, and, if those who led it were to remain loyal to their ideals, something more had to be done for them. They had been nearly three centuries handicapped by American slavery. Accordingly, when the Republican party was in control in the states as well as in the national govern-

1 Frederick Douglass, *The Life and Times of Frederick Douglass*, Centenary Memorial Suscribers' Edition, Pathway Press, New York, 1941, Appendix I, 649-50: an oration delivered on the occasion of the unveiling of the Freedman's Monument in memory of Abraham Lincoln, in Washington, D.C., April 4, 1876 (hereafter referred to as Douglass, *Life and Times*).

2 Lord Charnwood, *Abraham Lincoln*, Constable and Company, Ltd., London, 1917, 167. In speaking of Lincoln, Charnwood says: "The choice was not the result of merit; on the other hand, it was not the work of the ordinary wicked wirepuller, for what may be called the machine was working for Seward. The choice was made by plain representative Americans who set to themselves this question: 'With what candidate can we beat Douglas?' "

ment and when most of the southern whites had been disfranchised for having participated in the war against the Union, other steps were taken for the protection of the freedmen, among them being the Fourteenth Amendment.

By this measure a definition of citizenship was proclaimed; the rights and prerogatives of citizens were stipulated; and restrictions were placed upon the states forbidding them to deny or abridge those rights. When the language of this amendment is carefully scrutinized in the light of political situtions then existing throughout the world, it is hard to see anything left unsaid relative to the rights of citizens at that time. A citizen who meets specific objective qualifications may participate in the formation of the policies of his government and help in determination of its officers and offices. However, a new construction was to be placed upon the concept of citizenship, a construction which would make it possible for the South to prevent the freedmen from exercising the rights which the Fourteenth Amendment meant to confer. The Republicans, accordingly, made another effort to safeguard the rights which had been given to the freedmen by enacting the Fifteenth Amendment, forbidding the denial of the suffrage in any state to citizens on account of race, color or previous condition of servitude.

The Fifteenth Amendment was far-reaching in its implication and effects, for by it the Constitution was changed from what had been a states' rights document prior to the famous Sanford versus Scott decision in 1857[3] to a great charter of liberty. Then Frederick Douglass could say of the Republican party for having enacted the amendment, "It is in such humane acts that the glory and grandeur of the Grand Old Party lies."[4]

3 19 *Howard* 393.

4 Douglass, *Life and Times*, 650.

The objectives of the party were known to several important Negroes and to many of their white friends; consequently, recruiting new Negroes to the Republican fold was quite easy. The objectives appealed sufficiently strongly to retain those who were among the organizers of the party within its folds. Frederick Douglass declared that the Republican party was not only responsible for breaking the slavery bonds but it was also responsible for whatever progress the Negroes had made or would make in the immediate future. "The Republican party is the ship, all else the sea" was one of his favorite expressions.[5]

Since the Civil War, there have been times when the Republican party seemed recreant to its former traditions and those eternal principles of human liberty. Such an observation does not constitute in itself a sufficient reason for the Negro to change his allegiance and loyalty from it and to align himself with some other political party. Prior to 1936 the Democratic party had seldom shown any of the spirit of toleration or much of the milk of human kindness relative to the Negro in state and national affairs. Only the Republicans had done that. There were, however, a few isolated instances in a few cities or towns of the North of a Negro being given a position by the Democrats which carried fairly good pay and a little power and responsibility. The fact is that prior to 1924 no Negro was ever elected a delegate to the National Democratic Convention, and not one had ever been seated as a delegate by that body. However, in 1924 one was seated as a substitute in the Democratic Convention for a short time. This was the first time a Negro in the United States was so recognized by that party.[6]

All Negroes have never sanctioned all things done by the

5 *Ibid.*, 477-91.

6 *National Democratic Convention, Proceedings,* 1924, 62.

Republicans at all times, and neither have the Republicans always been just and upright in their dealing with the Negro. No one can deny, however, that the Negro was regarded as a personality by the Republicans in both the campaigns and the distribution of the spoils of victory, while he was completely neglected by the Democrats. There were some Negroes then who claimed that the methods employed by the Republicans to retain the Negroes' loyalty and support were not conducive to the general uplift and the best interest of the race.[7] One of the weaknesses of the policies of the Republican party, these claims is that it made available opportunities for a few party adherents to exploit other members of that race but did nothing for their general uplift. There were many Negroes who had demonstrated ability and capacity, and who would have been an asset to the Republicans had they been given an opportunity. This they were denied because of the Republicans' policies, because of inferior positions, indifference and deception. If sound policy had been followed, they argue, the Republican party would have had greater justification for expecting the loyal support of the Negro in the recent presidential elections (1936, 1940).

One finds much said about the abuse and misuse of the Negro in support of these contentions. Some of those complaints are old, occurring during the period of Reconstruction. Thus Honorable Hiram R. Revels, who represented Mississippi in the United States Senate, wrote to President Grant:

7 Joseph D. Bibbs, "Why I Am a Republican," letter to the writer, November 7, 1945; see Appendix 3. Attorney Bibbs, a Negro, is the grandson of the first governor of Alabama; he is a graduate of the Yale University Law School, and was for many years editor of the *Chicago Whip,* a popular Negro weekly newspaper. He is a member of the Illinois Bar, the Cook County Bar Association, and the Chicago Public Library Board.

> Since Reconstruction, the masses of my people have been, as it were, enslaved in mind to unprincipled adventurers, who caring nothing for the country, were willing to stoop to anything, no matter how infamous, to secure power for themselves and perpetuate it. My people are naturally Republicans, but as they grow older in freedom, so do they grow in wisdom. A great portion of them have learned that they are being used as tools, and, as in the late elections in Mississippi, not being able to correct the existing evils among themselves, they determined by casting their ballots against those unprincipled adventurers to overthrow them.[8]

Another former physician-politician declared, "The Republicans got the Negroes' support and then forgot them."[9]

If full weight and consideration to the claims of the Negroes were carefully analyzed and their grievances were set over against the efforts of the Republican party to enact beneficial measures, Negroes seem to have had little reason, if any, to indict and decry the activities of the Republican party prior to 1912. Those who were most articulate in making such charges seem to have ignored this fundamental fact: the politically innocent and inexperienced Negroes prior to 1920 had acquired no bargaining methods and techniques in politics, and what they called an abuse was a common practice of political parties toward an unorganized minority.

When the Republican party is looked at through the eyes of a social reformer of 1951, he sees its errors and recognizes some weaknesses and imperfections which its program contains.

8 Thomas A. Hendricks, "Retribution in Politics," *North American Review,* D. Appleton and Company, New York, CXXXVIII, 1879, 377-84.

9 Dr. E. E. Howard, letter, September 11, 1945; see Appendix 2.

Is there not a fallacy in judging the party by present-day demands and services relative to the value of its historical role toward the Negro? Would not more logic be employed if the programs and policies of the Republican party were compared and contrasted with the programs and policies of other parties then existing? Any unbiased and objective study of the platforms, speeches and public utterances of the leaders of the Republican party prior to 1932 would be filled with material indicating the Republican party was one of tolerance and sympathetic policies toward the Negro. This cannot be said of the Democratic party as we shall see in another chapter of this study.

The timely and appropriate question might be asked: What are some of the things which the Republican party has done or sponsored for the Negro? Were they not motivated in most of their efforts by considerations other than Negro uplift? Such a quantity of material has been produced by people representing so many points of view that one can find support of a kind for almost anything he wishes to prove. However, certain fundamental programs consistently sponsored by the Republicans tell their own story to any mind unclouded by prejudice or preconceived notions. One may start with the year 1857, only three years after the organization of the party in 1854, and he will find in Iowa, for example, that through the efforts of the Republican party the state convention submitted the question of Negro suffrage to popular vote. Although the measure was lost in Iowa it is significant to learn that over one fifth of the voters there supported it.[10] The evidence indicates that the Republicans were supported by the Free Soil party at the time. Again in Massachusetts as early as 1866 two Negroes were elected to the Assembly from the City of

10 G. C. Smith, *The Liberty and Free Soil Parties in the Northwest,* (no publisher given), New York, 1897, 23-41.

Boston: E. G. Walker and Charles L. Mitchell, both on the Republican ticket.[11] In 1869 Ebenezer Don Carlos of Philadelphia, Pennsylvania, was appointed minister resident and consul general to Haiti by a Republican President and Senate, he being the first Negro appointed by the United States government to such a position.[12] The above facts are illustrative, at least in part, of the attitude and policy of the Republican party toward the Negro, an attitude which it seems was one of genuine tolerance and uplift.

Added significance is given this situation when those facts are set over against the attitude and policy of the rival party during the same period, 1865-1932. It would probably aid in gaining a true perspective were one to keep in mind that whatever policies were initiated in the South relative to the Negro were effected by the Democratic party, except during the carpetbaggers' regime, 1870-1877. It was the Democrats who were in power in the South most of the time.

Throughout the period in which the Democratic party dominated the political thought and behavior of the South, one notices that the southern states not only refused to accept any degree of tolerance toward the Negro but at one time they defiantly rejected the Federal Constitution.[13] The situation in both the White House and Congress was tense after weeks of debate over the matter, so tense as to bring forth a joint appeal by both President and Congress for the voters to decide by election the method of admitting those states to the Union.[14] The decision reached was: The rebellious states

11 C. F. Bishop, *History of Election in American Colonies,* "Columbia University Studies in History," Volume III, New York, 1893, 7-97.

12 *Ibid.,* 193.

13 *Political Science Quarterly,* edited by Faculty of Political Science, Columbia College, New York, Volume IX, 1894, 680-86.

14 *Congressional Globe,* Part I, 39th Congress, 2d Session, Washington, D.C., Volume XXXVII, 1866-67, 16 ff.

were to ratify the Fifteenth Amendment. Despite this, the southern states defied the congressional mandate for, when their legislatures met, each state selected a different date to act on the amendment.[15]

That the purpose of the Fifteenth Amendment was the general uplift of the Negro is a fact that no one can deny, hence any effort to reject this amendment can only be construed as having been an effort to deny Negroes the benefits which it carried. Thus, while the Republicans were endeavoring to increase the political status of the Negro, the Democrats were endeavoring to decrease it or, at most, to preserve the *status quo.* Their efforts, attitudes and position have been clearly stated by one of America's foremost historians:

> Most of the states presented in one way or another the reasons for their actions. Objection was made to the constitutional amendment when ten southern states were unrepresented in Congress, and also the menace of a reduced representation, but the most formidable obstacle to ratification lay in the so called penal section which disfranchised from holding office the political leaders of the South. The Southern people, it was said, were asked to be instruments of their dishonor by fastening a stigma upon men who had their sympathy and whom they had followed with pride. The Amendment is "an insulting outrage," declared the Governor of Mississippi. "It is a denial of equal rights of many of our worthiest citizens."[16]

Here one sees that the policy of the Democratic party was

15 M. N. Work, *The Negro Yearbook,* 1922, 175.

16 James Ford Rhodes, *History of the United States from the Compromise of 1850,* The Macmillan Company, New York, 1909, Volume VII, 6-8.

almost anything but democratic. That attitude may be contrasted with the attitude and policy during that same period of the Republican party, which was accepting Negro delegates in the National Convention, using them on different committees in the national campaigns, electing them to national offices, and appointing them to national positions of power, responsibility, deference and influence. The record of the Republican party is replete with examples of its efforts to uplift the Negro. However, there were a few Republicans who had much to say about the soundness of the Negro's preparation for use of the elective franchise.[17] It would probably be illustrative and informative to mention briefly some of the Negroes who held positions of weight and responsibility in the Republican councils.

As early as 1868 there were Negro delegates in the Republican convention: James Harris of North Carolina and P. B. S. Pinchback of Louisiana.[18] In 1872, several other states sent Negro delegates to the National Convention. Included among the delegates were A. J. Ransier and Robert Small of South Carolina; B. K. Bruce and J. R. Lynch of Mississippi; William H. Grey of Arkansas; William H. Gibson and J. T. Walls of Florida.[19] In subsequent conventions, there were James T. Rapier and B. P. Turner of Alabama;[20] M. W. Gibbs of Arkansas;[21] G. M. Wilder and E. H. Deas of South Carolina;[22] John C. Dancy, H. P. Cheatham, J. E. O'Hara and G. C. Scurlock of North Carolina;[23] J. C. Napier of Tennessee;[24] C. H. Payne of West Virginia and John M. Langston of

17 *Congressional Globe,* XL, 1868, 180 ff.
18 *Republican National Convention, Proceedings,* 1868, 115.
19 *Ibid.,* 1872, 184-186.
20 *Ibid.,* 1876, 340.
21 *Ibid.,* 1884, 340.
22 *Ibid.,* 64.
23 *Ibid.,* 1888, 89-105.
24 *Ibid.,* 1896, 104-105.

Virginia;[25] Judson Lyons and Jon Long of Florida;[26] Walter Cohen and S. W. Green of Louisiana;[27] and N. W. Cuney of Texas:[28] a partial list of Negro delegates in attendance at Republican conventions prior to 1900. One searches in vain for a single Negro delegate to any of the Democratic National Conventions at this time (1865-1900). Indeed, there was not only an absence of Negroes, but any white man who suggested reforms in the Democratic party which would make Negro delegates possible was referred to by the opprobrious term "nigger lover" and the reformer's place was likely to be occupied by another white man in subsequent conventions.

The contrast in the attitude and policies of the two major parties was sufficient to drive the Negro to the Republican party and away from the Democratic party, had he been inclined toward the Democratic.

A study of the contested delegations at some of the Republican conventions removes any doubt of this fact. The contested delegation resulted from a split in the control of the Republican party or from the existence of two factions in the party, each of which claimed to be the true representatives of the party in its state. One faction, a mixed or bi-racial group, was called "Black and Tan"; the other, an all-white group, was called "Lily White." Because the whites of the South have been Democratic in their party affiliation since the Civil War, the Republican party in the South has been largely composed of Negroes, and controlled by them. Reflection and observation upon that situation gave birth to the idea that a change of its Negro personnel for a white or mixed one would strengthen the Republicans in the South and destroy the one-party system

25 *Ibid.*, 66.
26 *Ibid.*, 1884, 65.
27 *Ibid.*, 1884, 67.
28 *Ibid.*, 1880, 310.

there. Many white Republicans thought the idea was feasible. In pursuit of such a belief there emerged a group of whites who set as their immediate political objective to obtain control of the Republican machine in the South and, subsequently, to distribute the patronage. "It was consideration of patronage that led many southern whites to align themselves with the Republican party in the South."[29]

The contested delegation in 1912 and the split in the Republican party, one faction of which was led by William Howard Taft, the other (called "Bull Moose"[30]) by Theodore Roosevelt, did not adversely affect the loyalty of the Negro to the party's principles. Negroes as a group remained Republican; however, some of them supported Taft, while others supported Roosevelt. There is nothing in the election returns indicating the Negro's support of the Democratic candidate.

Too much emphasis cannot be put on the fact that Negro delegates at Republican conventions prior to 1916 were from the South. The northern Negroes then were not sufficiently concentrated, nor organized, nor politically alert to have many Negro delegates. Since 1916, however, there have been an increasing number of Negro delegates to the Republican National Convention from the North. This situation was largely the result of the migration of large numbers of Negroes to the North, beginning in that year. (See Chapter II.)

One finds evidence of the political significance of the migra-

29 *Chicago Defender*, May 2, 1932, quoting from William L. MacDonald of Fort Worth, Texas. Mr. MacDonald has been for several years the National Committeeman of the Republican party from Texas, and a delegate to several of the national conventions.

30 When the progressive Republicans declared themselves opposed to the renomination of President Taft, and brought about a three-cornered election, the "bull moose" became a very useful symbol as opposed to the elephant of the regular Republicans and the donkey of the Democrats.

tion when, in 1916, W. F. Cozart was a delegate to the convention from the Second District of New Jersey, a district which included Atlantic City;[31] in 1924, Dr. G. E. Cannon was delegate-at-large to the National Republican Convention from Jersey City, New Jersey,[32] and in 1928, Dr. W. E. Alexander was delegate-at-large from Orange, New Jersey, along with W. E. Edge,[33] In 1920, there was one Negro delegate to the Republican National Convention from Illinois, Oscar DePriest;[34] in 1924, Illinois sent two Negro delegates, DePriest and Louis B. Anderson, with one alternate, Dan Jackson.[35] In 1928, the Seventy-first District of Ohio sent L. N. Bundy of Cleveland as delegate to the convention. Thus, one sees many Negroes from northern states in attendance at the Republican Convention after the migration of large numbers of their group to the North.

These data illustrate to some extent the consideration which the Republicans gave to the Negro. It was such consideration, at least in part, which caused the Republicans to hold sway over the Negro's political loyalties for over a half century after their emancipation. In addition to permitting the Negro to participate in the conventions and the campaigns, another consideration of the Republicans is worthy of notice, for it went far toward tying the Negro to the party.

Whenever the party was victorious in elections, a few Negroes were given conspicuous positions. As an illustration the names and positions held by some Negroes at various times are here given: W. T. Vernon of Kansas and J. C. Napier of Tennessee, Registrars of the Treasury; Frederick Douglass of

31 *Republican National Convention, Proceedings,* 1916, 54.
32 *Ibid.,* 1924, 69.
33 *Ibid.,* 1928, 84.
34 *Ibid.,* 1920, 48.
35 *Ibid.,* 1924, 73.

Maryland and Henry L. Judson of Georgia, Recorder of Deeds of the District of Columbia; William H. Lewis of Massachusetts, Assistant Attorney General of the United States; Ralph W. Tyler of Ohio, Auditor for the Navy Department; Winfield McKinley, Collector of Customs of the District of Columbia; Charles W. Anderson, Collector of Internal Revenue, New York City; S. L. Williams, Special Assistant, United States District Attorney at Chicago; Dr. William D. Crum, Collector of the Port at Charleston, South Carolina; Walter Cohen, Collector of the Port at New Orleans; Judson Lyons, Postmaster at Savannah, Georgia. Booker T. Washington, while not officially holding an appointive position, was nevertheless an adviser to President Roosevelt.[36] Every one of these appointments was obtained under Republican administrations, and every one terminated when a Democratic administration succeeded a Republican.

The elective offices which Negroes held under Republican administrations constitute an imposing list, ranging all the way from Justice of Peace in some rural backward areas to twenty-two members of the House of Representatives and two United States Senators.[37] In both appointive and elective offices, Negroes have held places on some of the important Convention committees, such as the following: (1) Permanent Organizations; (2) Credentials; (3) Rules and Order; (4) Resolutions.[38] Indeed, there was one Negro governor, P. B. S. Pinchback of Louisiana; and, in 1884, John R. Lynch of Missississippi was temporary chairman of the National Convention. It was reliably reported that had Lynch's delegation in 1880 and the delegations of other southern and northern states not yielded in the interest

36 M. N. Work, *The Negro Yearbook*, volume for 1910-28.

37 Samuel Denny Smith, *The Negro in Congress, 1870-1901*, University of North Carolina Press, Chapel Hill, N. C., 1940, 5.

38 Republican National Conventions, 1872, 1884, 1888, 1896, and 1900.

of party unity in 1884, B. K. Bruce, an able senator from Mississippi, would have been selected as the party's nominee for Vice-President of the United States. Thereby the Negro would have been given a higher position than he had previously held.[39]

Positions and deference in the Republican party such as have been previously described led some Negroes to think of being identified with the Republican party as an attainment of honor, for it was the party of reforms, tolerance and uplift. Another line of thought led Negroes to believe the Democratic party represented intolerance, disfranchisement, segregation, lynching, and everything opposed to their best interest. Hence it was considered a sign of dishonor and backwardness to be identified with that party.[40] It was said of Negroes who identified themselves with the Democratic party that they endorsed the things done by the southern Democrats and the policies they fostered.[41] The charge was weighty, since most of the obstructions to their progress, they were told, had been the result of the cunning, conniving and wicked practices of the Democrats. The Negro, being unable to analyze or to appreciate the difference between true and false doctrines, accepted much that was false about the political parties. Since the Republicans were first to secure the Negroes' confidence and allegiance, they were more effective with their false pro-

39 J. R. Lynch, *Facts of Reconstruction,* Neal Publishing Company, New York, 1913, 6.

40 *Ibid.,* 77-79.

41 *Chicago Bee,* May 11, 1932, quoting Robert R. Church, who was the National Republican Committeeman of Tennessee for several years (1924-1940). Oscar DePriest, a former member of the House of Representatives, a delegate to the National Republican Convention several times from Illinois, and a former Alderman and Ward Committeeman in Chicago, made this comment to the writer about Negro Democrats, "There is a melancholy fate awaiting any man who compromises with the devil. To the Negro, devils and Democrats are two names for the same thing" (November 2, 1945).

paganda with Negroes than were their rivals, the Democrats.

Another factor of importance in making the Negroes Republicans and in sustaining them in the party was the oratory of some of the Negro adherents. Those orators, when speaking to Negro audiences, stressed the point that the G.O.P. was the party which gave them citizenship, the ballot, public office, and other forms of deference. Roscoe Conklin Simmons (reputed to be one of the greatest orators in the United States) in a speech supporting Hoover's candidacy for re-election in 1932 declared:

> If you put a Democrat in the White House, you put the Negro again into virtual slavery. They [Democrats] have neither the brains to run this country nor the sense of decency to be fair and just to you.

A little later (in that speech) he declared:

> I'll say the Republicans built this country: I'll say even more than that: I'll say the Republicans built this country largely upon your shoulders. Now do you want to tear down or to be a party to those who will tear down what you have built up through work, blood, tears and prayers? I am sure you hold sacred the suffering of your forefathers who bought this privilege for you by giving their last full measure of devotion for it [voting] and that you will treat it as an hallowed trust. Hoover is the representative of the party and the principles of our forefathers and your best interest.[42]

42 *Chicago Defender*, October 28, 1932. Also, *Chicago Bee*, October 25, 1932. Colonel Roscoe Conklin Simmons was a member of the Republican Speaker's Committee in 1932; in 1936 it was he who seconded the nomination of Alfred M. Landon for the presidency at the Republican Convention in Cleveland, Ohio.

Many expressions in the speech may not be historically correct but most of the people in a political meeting are not as much concerned about technical history as they are about the record, the justification and policies of their candidate and party; and the deficiency and condemnation of the policies and candidate of the rival party. Therefore, such oratory as is frequently employed by Republicans wields a strong influence in keeping the Negro in the Republican party. It is impossible to say which has been most effective—what Negroes saw in the forms of jobs, policies and constructive legislation, or what they *heard* in terms of praise and compliments of them and the Republicans or condemnation of the Democrats in sustaining them in the Republican camps.

It is a common observation that climax and decline are two different parts of the same action. When the Republican party reached a position in which it could render its maximum service to the causes of Negro uplift, then the forces of disintergration set in. These forces made it appear that the Republicans had forgotten their earlier policies, pledges and traditions.

The Negro was a long time in realizing that the Republican party had slipped from some of its traditional democratic moorings and was drifting into the muddy waters of plutocracy. The *New York Age,* a militant Negro weekly, took notice of that tendency as early as 1907 and declared editorially:

> The politicians that we have known and with whom we have been in active sympathy . . . with here and there a discordant note for the past quarter of a century, with the policies they have stood for in party management and the conduct of the government, have passed out of active control of Republican politics

> in the state and in the nation. The Republican party has ceased to be the champion of the American democracy of the 1850's, '60's and '70's. It has become a mere political machine.[43]

The editorial contains a long discussion on traditional Republican policies and concludes:

> They [the Negroes] cannot do in the future as they have done in the past without wrecking their citizenship. It would be futile to form a race party. It would be folly to go boldly from the Republican to the Democratic party. But if they should give support to one party or another as it shows a disposition to be genuinely democratic, regardless of race in its principles and policies, they [the Negroes] would find the support of their race largely sought for by both parties.[44]

Another example of awareness of the Republican's indifference toward the Negro was demonstrated in 1912 when William Monroe Trotter, editor and publisher of the popular and liberal *Boston Guardian,* a Negro weekly, called upon Woodrow Wilson, the Democratic candidate for the presidency that year, and offered to support him if he would, on being elected, sponsor some legislation favorable to the Negro race and give to the Negro leaders some consideration in distributing the spoils.[45] This was not the first example of Negroes offering their service to a Democratic candidate, as we shall see in the next chapter. This offer by William Monroe Trotter is

43 *New York Age,* Fred R. Moore Corporation, New York, October 23, 1907, 1.

44 *Ibid.,* 2.

45 *The Nation,* The Nation's Press, New York, Volume XC, 1918, 606 ff.

unique, however, in light of what President Taft in his administration just ending had said. Trotter's bolt of the party implied that if the Republicans were to continue to influence the political behavior of the Negro they (Republicans) would have to pay a better price for their support than they were then paying, or the Negro would support parties and men who would.

Other evidence of the Negro's bolt of the Republican party is noticed in 1912 when the party held its National Convention in Chicago. The Reverend Reverdy C. Ransom, who later became a Bishop in the African Methodist Episcopal Church, took President William Howard Taft to task, charging him with having reversed the policies of President Theodore Roosevelt and all of his Republican predecessors when he (President Taft) initiated a policy of refusing to Negroes positions in a community where the whites did not like such an appointment. He charged the President with insulting the race on two occasions at least: first, when the President remained silent about lynching after his nomination until the beginning of his campaign for election; and secondly, when the President addressed the students and faculty at Wilberforce University and expressed a belief that all education should be "Jim Crowed."

Following these carefully worded charges Reverend Ransom pointed out that insult was not the worst charge to be filed against the President. A worse charge against him was his failure to keep his promises. For example, he promised to make Mr. J. C. Napier Treasurer of the United States, but instead tried to appease Mr. Napier and the Negro race by making him Registrar of the Treasury. The position which had been promised to Napier was given to a white man. From the Negro's point of view this was a most damaging charge against the President: for as one prominent Negro politician commented, "It made some of the Negroes believe that Mr. Taft was a wolf dressed in sheep's clothes."[46] Reverend Ransom strengthened his attack on Mr. Taft when he pointed out that Mr. Taft had totally and completely disregarded the interest of the Negro race again when the President indicated his intention of appointing to the Supreme Court Judge Hook, known to be anti-Negro in everything uplifting, as Judge Hook had clearly shown his attitude as co-author of an infamous Jim Crow decision.[47] After having heard those charges, a group of politicians referred to as the "Black Cabinet," because they advised the President on matters relative to the Negro, went to the President and told him that if he carried out his plan to appoint Judge Hook no Negro of note would speak in his favor in the campaign.[48]

Many Negro leaders began to accuse the Republicans of turning over the patronage of the South to the whites. This meant that the Negro was no longer being considered as a politically valuable group to be reckoned with by the Republican party. In 1912 a small group of Negroes conceived the idea of interesting far-seeing Democrats in them; and since Woodrow Wilson, they thought, was a new type of politician, he was the man who could effect such an alliance with the northern Democrats. That situation would result in dividing the northern Negro vote and in bringing into the South a

46 *New York Age,* October 3, 1912, quoting William Monroe Trotter.

47 "Negroes in the Republican Convention," *The Nation,* Volume CXIV, 1912, 606. One finds there an excellent discussion of that convention. This is the only reference that the writer was able to find to Judge Hook or the decision about which Reverend Ransom had so much to say. Because of the paucity of data on either the Judge or the infamous decision, Reverend Ransom's charge here seemed to be without factual support and merit.

48 *Ibid.,* 606.

real government of the people. Bishop Alexander Waters of the African Methodist Episcopal Church wrote to President Wilson outlining the plan. In reply, President Wilson stated that:

> [It was his] earnest wish to see justice done the Negro people in every matter; and not mere grudging justice, but justice with liberality and cordial good feeling.[49]

A similar move which grew out of an attitude of indifference by the Republican party was responsible for large numbers of Negroes voting Democratic in the election of 1912, for there was nothing in the platform of the Progressive party under the domination of Theodore Roosevelt to indicate its willingness to revive the Republican tradition of friendliness and helpfulness to the Negro. In fact, a group of Negroes, including the foremost leaders in civic and educational circles, met with Mr. Roosevelt at the National Progressive Convention and insisted upon his incorporating in the platform a plank declaring "the Progressive party recognizes that distinction of race or class in political life has no place in a democracy."[50] This was turned down. Woodrow Wilson's election followed the split in the Republican party in 1912, but in 1916 it was thought by most political observers that the Negro vote went solidly for Hughes.[51]

In the campaign of 1920 the Negro's support went almost solidly for the Republican candidate, Warren G. Harding. Since the campaign did not create much excitement among

49 W. E. B. DuBois, "The Republicans and the Black Voter," *The Nation,* The Nation's Press, New York, June 5, 1920, 757.

50 *Ibid.,* 758.

51 J. G. Van Deusen, *The Black Man in White America,* Associated Publishers, Washington, D.C., 1938, Chapter IX.

Negroes, it can be passed over here. It contributed little, if anything, toward changing their political thought. However, Harding's administration was a different story. He not only failed to appoint any Negro to a position of honor and responsibility but he failed also to give public censure to social and political conditions of the South in reference to the Negro. In fact, he seems to have endorsed the southern attitude in a speech of October 26, 1921, at Birmingham, Alabama. Some Negroes interpreted his speech as fostering the southern racial policy.[52]

There were two expressions to which the Negro took exception: first, "I plead with my own political party to lay aside any program that looks to lining up the black man as a mere political adjunct"; and secondly, "There is a fundamental, eternal and inescapable difference between the Negro and the white man." Some of the comments of the Negro press bespeak eloquently their attitude about the speech. A few liked part of the speech, but most of them seemed to like none of it.

The *New York News,* a Negro weekly, declared:

> None of our Presidents have exhibited such moral courage in pleading for just treatment of the Negro, in the section where that quality has been so severely lacking.[53]

One's attention is called to the fact that this was a comment upon the speech as a whole and has no reference to its objectionable features.

52 *Chicago Defender,* November 3, 1921; *The Crisis,* December, 1921.

53 George W. Harris, editor, New York News Publishing Company, New York, November 3, 1921.

The *Baltimore Afro-American,* also a Negro weekly, editorially commented:

> The President's Birmingham speech is being criticized because it promised the colored race too little, and by the white people because it promised so much.[54]

The Crisis, a monthly magazine, editorially declared:

> Mr. Harding meant that the American Negro must acknowledge that it was a wrong and a disgrace for Booker T. Washington to dine with President Roosevelt. The answer to this inconceivably dangerous and undemocratic demand must come with the unanimous ring of twelve million voices, enforced by the vote of every American who believes in humanity.[55]

The *New York Crusade,* a Negro monthly newspaper, declared:

> The President's speech supports the worst negro-phobist element of the South on at least six vital points: first, the denial of social equality; secondly, the plan of supporting such Negro leaders as will acquiesce in this denial, and in utilizing Negro schools as will further increase the number; thirdly, the claim of inherent Negro inferiority; fourthly, the unwritten southern law that "black men cannot be white men," which after elimination of color changes as a recognized

54 Afro-American Publishing Company, Baltimore, November 2, 1921.
55 Official Organ of the National Association for the Advancement of Colored People, New York, November 1, 1921.

> impossibility, simply means that black men cannot expect to enjoy all the rights and privileges of American citizenship, enjoyed by white men, citizens and aliens; fifthly, the South's plan for exclusive industrial education as against any higher education for Negroes; sixthly, the South's noisy opposition to racial amalgamation while silently indulging in its practice.[56]

The *Associated Negro Press* through its *Department of Public Opinion Bulletin* said:

> There are two features of the address that have come in for more comment than any of the others. The two are "Political Equality" and "Social Equality."
>
> The discussion of the "Social Equality" portion of the address has been very exclusive within the group, as well as without. There is a great difference of opinion concerning the advisability of this reference. Dr. DuBois, Dr. Kelly Miller, as the intellectual group are in the section of those who think social reference in the address was untimely, and yet insist, since the reference is made, there should be no barrier set up by a nation, or individual, seeking to dictate the policy of social selection between individuals.

A little further the release continues:

> There has seemed to be no more excitement and alarm, by both races, on this phase of the President's address than any other. It is noticeable that the active political group, headed up by R. R. Church, Henry Lincoln

56 November 2, 1921.

> Johnson, Perry W. Howard, Walter Cohen and others in the Republican party accept the address as a masterpiece of carefully expressed opinion.[57]

Those excerpts and comments indicate that shapers of Negro political thought interpreted the President's position at best to be one of compromise with the South on social and political matters. His position left no good blood in the veins of the Negro for him.[58] Several Negro politicians believe that if Mr. Harding had lived and had been the Republican nominee for the presidency in 1924 to succeed himself, the Negro would not have given him enthusiastic support.[59]

During the Coolidge regime the Negro had very little against which to register political complaint. The country enjoyed a period of prosperity. The Negro was employed and was making more money in this country than ever before in peacetime. There were fewer race riots than in the period 1920-1924, and the number of Negroes lynched had declined.[60] The Negro credited the Republicans and Mr. Coolidge with this and hence felt no reason to revolt. An analysis of the election returns from districts preponderantly Negro indicates that other than a few votes given to Senator LaFollette of Wisconsin in 1924 the Republicans received most of the Negro's support.[61] An examination of the Negro weekly newspapers gives further credence to this belief; nearly all of note supported the Republican candidate, a few were lukewarm toward the

57 See *Chicago Defender,* November 3, 1921; *Kansas City Call,* Kansas City Call, Inc., Kansas City, Mo., November 3, 1921.

58 *Opportunity,* January, 1922.

59 *Black Despatch,* January 2, 1923; *New York News,* January 9, 1923; *The Crisis,* December, 1924, 16-27.

60 *Negro Yearbook,* 1924; 1928, 19 ff.

61 *World Almanac,* 1925, 724-735.

Progressive nominee, but not one is noted for the Democratic nominee.[62]

The Hoover nomination made after Coolidge's famous expression in the South Dakota Black Hills, "I do not choose to run," was at first given support by the Negro Republican politicians; but when the Democratic nominee of 1928 outlined his program and straightforwardly expressed his policies, Negroes began to increase in number in the latter camp. An examination of the Negro press reveals about as much space given to Governor Alfred E. Smith of New York as to the California engineer, Herbert C. Hoover.

The office-holding and office-seeking Negro Republicans as usual used their influence for the nomination of Mr. Hoover in the Republican National Convention, and after his nomination they struggled more untiringly for his election. However, those who had no political axe to grind, those who remembered the food shortage of World War I, those who questioned Mr. Hoover's eligibility under the qualifying clauses of the Constitution, since he had been out of continental United States for more than fourteen consecutive years, and, further, those who could see Governor Alfred E. Smith as one identified with a minority, if not in racial origin at least in religion, felt none too warmly inclined toward Mr. Hoover.

By 1928, Negroes in the United States were more politically alert than ever before. This was due, in part, to their penetration into the North and to participation in politics there. They were taught not only to expect more from politics in terms of deference and responsibility, but, if necessary, to demand

62 The following were consulted: *Kansas City Call,* June-November, 1924; *Baltimore Afro-American,* June-November, 1924; *Pittsburgh Courier,* November, 1924; *New York Age,* June-November, 1924; *Chicago Defender,* June-November, 1924; *Cleveland Plain Dealer,* June-November, 1924; *St. Louis Argus,* June-November, 1924.

more.[63] Accordingly, when Herbert Hoover became the standard-bearer of the Republican party, some of the Negro leaders sent out a barrage of questions to the chairman of the National Convention and to the several National Committeemen of the respective states demanding to know where Mr. Hoover stood on the question of patronage and what was his program for their economic, social and political uplift.[64] It seems that Negroes had firmly resolved not to support blindly a man simply because he happened to wear a Republican label. Mr. Hoover was asked to make his position clear in his acceptance speech. After a committee of prominent Negroes waited on him, Mr. Hoover agreed to comply with the request.[65] In his acceptance speech, among other things, Mr. Hoover said:

> There is one of the ideals of America upon which I wish at this time to lay especial emphasis, for we should constantly test our economic, social, and governmental system by certain ideas that must control them. The founders of our Republic pronounced the revolutionary doctrine that all men are created equal and that all men should have equality before the law.

Mr. Hoover then carefully traced the development of the concept of equality and its application to concrete situations in the United States by declaring:

> It was Abraham Lincoln who firmly enunciated this ideal as the equality clause . . . While the Negro as an

63 Speech by Commissioner Edward H. Wright, *Chicago Defender,* October 25, 1926.

64 *Ibid.,* July 29, 1928. Also, *Pittsburgh Courier,* July 22, 1928.

65 *Chicago Bee,* August 18, 1928. Also, *Baltimore Afro-American,* August 25, 1928.

> American citizen is interested in all of the issues of this campaign, he must of necessity first get freely and fully the equality of opportunity with all other American citizens before he can fully appreciate, participate, and enjoy his full citizenship rights; to attain equality of opportunity will be to remove all other disabilities.[66]

The pronouncement was by far more considerate of the Negro than any which had been made by a Republican presidential candidate since Theodore Roosevelt; however, it was not sufficient to command the united and full support of the Negro. It was not a question of what Mr. Hoover had done or would do as it was the bids of the Democrats and the personality of their nominee, Governor Alfred E. Smith.

Not only did Negroes admire Smith for the liberal reforms initiated while he was governor of the Empire State but also for his sympathy for the underprivileged.[67] Governor Smith was a part of the powerful New York Tammany machine which had shown a spirit of tolerance and uplift toward the Negro on several occasions. Indeed, several years prior to 1928, Tammany Hall had intensively cultivated the Harlem district and had gone out for Negro votes. It had given a number of Negroes unique positions, and built up a reputation among them for keeping its campaign promises. In that campaign Tammany had promised to double the number of positions held by Negroes, which promise led many Negroes to think that were Governor Smith elected president he would continue that liberal policy toward them.[68] Governor Smith was truthful and fearless.

A comparison of the public records of the rival candidates

66 *Chicago Tribune,* August 17, 1928.
67 *The Crisis,* October, 1928.
68 *New York Age,* September 1, 1928.

caused some Negroes to ponder whether to support Smith or Hoover. The Negro seemed to have been confronted with a problem similar to that confronting Shakespeare's Hamlet: "To be or not to be" a Republican or a Democrat was his question in this campaign.

Both of the major parties showed much concern about the Negro vote and the best means to employ in order to recruit it and keep it. It was generally thought the contest would be close and it was not unthinkable that the Negro in certain pivotal states might constitute the balance of power.

Thus F. R. Kent, a close observer of political trends, declared:

> The Republicans and Democrats are both worried, and no small part of their worry is caused by the uncertainty regarding the colored brother's vote. Meanwhile the political doctors are frantically prescribing.[69]

Then followed a lengthy discussion of the loyalty of the Negro to the Republican party in which Mr. Kent showed why the Republicans had just cause to worry at the time:

> They won't admit this publicly, but privately, the more candid of the so-called party leaders say that there are certain menacing signs, not lightly to be ignored, that a lot of money and work will be necessary to keep the Negro a permanent cornerstone of the "G.O.P."[70]

Bishop W. T. Vernon, former Registrar of the Treasury as well as twice president of Western University, a Negro college

69 *Collier's*, New York, Volume LXXXII, October 20, 1928, 13.
70 *Ibid.*, 14.

in Quindaro, Kansas, said of the campaign, "Hoover had Esau's voice while Smith had Jacob's hand, and the Negro was called upon to decide whether his cause would be advanced by words or deeds."[71]

A careful analysis of the election returns for 1924 and 1926 leads one to the conviction that the Negroes in Harlem gave Governor Smith a large vote in those years. Every district dominated by Negroes turned in a substantial plurality for Smith.

In the contest and campaign for the nation's highest honor in 1928 no one could give a good reason why the Negro then should not support Governor Smith. Indeed one may find many reasons for expecting the Negro to support him in preference to Mr. Hoover: first, Governor Smith was known to favor a repeal of the Prohibition Amendment and the Negroes were generally in favor of its repeal; secondly, Governor Smith was an uncompromising foe of the Ku Klux Klan and the Negroes thought a vote for him was a vote against the Klan. Hoover's position on each of these issues was vague. Thirdly, it was repeatedly pointed out that Mr. Hoover was giving support to a "Lily White" Republican party in the South from which Negroes were eliminated and that a vote for him was a sanction of the Democratic party's politics in the South: more lynching, more segregation, more hard times.[72] When those facts and charges were put before the Negro public it ceased to be a question of speculation whether Negroes, though traditionally Republican in the South, would become Democrats in the North. Four years later, 1932, they not only did support Governor Franklin D. Roosevelt in large numbers in preference to President Hoover, but also an increas-

71 See the *Kansas City Call,* June 6, 1932.

72 Associated Negro Press release in the *Pittsburgh Courier,* Pittsburgh Courier Publishing Company, Pittsburgh, October 27, 1928.

ing number adopted the slogans, "Anybody but Hoover" or "Who but Hoover," which were current then.[73]

That campaign and election sent the Negro's political stock skyward; many careful political observers believed that if Governor Smith could carry the South he would need the votes of only a few northern states where the Negroes were concentrated to win the election, such as New York, Illinois, Pennsylvania, and Indiana.[74] Because of the strategic position which the Negro had attained in the political affairs of the nation, both of the political parties met promise with promise, concession with concession, bid with bid, and money with money.

The Republicans, in an effort to recruit new Negro votes as well as to retain old ones, resorted to a trite trick of propaganda. They obtained the services of a prominent Negro physician-politician, Dr. J. R. Hawkins, the Negro who later seconded Mr. Hoover's nomination in Kansas City in 1932. He was put in charge of a division at the Republican National Headquarters and from that position he declared that one of the immediate aims of Mr. Hoover was to break down "Jim Crow" laws in Virginia and throughout the nation.[75] Anyone with one ounce of political intelligence knew this statement must be untrue, for no one man in the United States, though he be President, could alone change the southern policies.

The Democrats were not slow in the use of propaganda in an effort to recruit new Negro support. One example will suffice

73 "Who But Hoover," *Collier's*, Volume LXXXVI, 1932, 12. Attorney L. B. Moore, former Assistant Attorney-General of the State of Illinois, who was a member of the Roosevelt-for-President Committee of 1932, declared in an interview that Hoover's name had become opprobrious to all the best-thinking Negroes before his term was over. In several of the speeches which Attorney Moore made against the re-election of Hoover, he frequently emphasized the phrase, "Who but Hoover."

74 *Chicago Bee*, August 25, 1928, quoting Dr. W. E. B. DuBois.

75 *Ibid.*, November 3, 1928.

to illustrate the point. In Chicago the beautiful Savoy Ballroom was the scene of a gathering of a large number of the nation's most publicized Negroes. The purpose of the meeting was to clarify the issues in the campaign and indicate to the Negroes which of the candidates had their interest most in mind. Attorney Clarence Darrow, who was a member of the National Association for the Advancement of Colored People, was to speak on the program. He had endeared himself to the Negro by his brilliant defense of Dr. O. H. Sweet, who had slain several whites in Detroit when they had attempted to force him to abandon his home.

The meeting was sponsored by the Honorable A. W. Scott, Past Grand Exalted Ruler of the Imperial Benevolent and Protective Order of the Elks of the World; the Honorable William H. Wallace, High Commissioner of the Universal Negro Improvement Association; the Reverend Noah H. Williams, pastor of the St. Paul African Methodist Episcopal Church of St. Louis; the Reverend S. E. Maloney, pastor, Allen Temple African Methodist Episcopal Church, Chicago; Attorney Earl B. Dickerson, a popular, brilliant young lawyer of Chicago; and Dr. O. H. Sweet of Detroit. The advertisement of the meeting promised "free ice cream and music," both magnetic in drawing Negro crowds.

At the meeting Hoover was denounced as a faker, a former Democrat, an opportunist, a tool of Wall Street, a southern sympathizer, an oppressor of minorities, and a man without a program. Smith, on the other hand, was extolled to the skies.[76] There is no way of determining the number of votes the meeting secured for Governor Smith. The size of the crowd, which was very large, as well as the exhibition of enthusiasm, would indicate Smith was very popular and this popularity did not suffer

76 *Chicago Bee,* October 24, 1928; also November 3, 1928.

as a result of the meeting. The campaign was a hotly contested one. There was bitter personal criticism by each of the opponents. Some campaign managers believe, however, that such criticism does a candidate more good than harm. A striking illustration is found in the gubernatorial campaign of 1926 when Al Smith made the most of Ogden Mills' charge that he could not be trusted either in public or in private life. In a reply to this accusation, Smith stated:

> Twenty-seven years ago I knelt before the altar . . . and in the presence of God Almighty promised to care for, honor, and protect the woman of my choice. And if I suddenly was ushered tonight before the Great White Throne I would be prepared to establish that I had kept that promise. Let the Congressman lay his private life along side of mine.[77]

Smith, by that act, seems to have won so much public sympathy that his rival was forced to retract his accusations.

Hoover was an artist in the use of weighted words. The following excerpts, taken almost at random from a collection of his speeches, illustrate the fact:

> We must have emancipation from the creeping collectivism of dictated economy. We must take the government out of business in competition with the citizens. We must have freedom of business, labor and farmers from government dictation. We must grant genuine relief to farmers and restore the farmer's judgment in control of his business. We must have reform in the Labor act to deal equal justice to all workers and all

77 Peter Odegard, *The American Public Mind,* Columbia University Press, New York, 1930, 160-61.

> employers. We must have the only basis of liberalism, that is the rule of law and not of men. We must reform relief under the administration of non-partisan local committees. We must reform the old age pensions to make them just to the workers. We need to adopt real measures which enable people to obtain better housing. We must advance the whole question of medical attention to the indigent.[78]

Consider the phrases: "creeping collectivism," "dictated economy," "government dictation," "equal justice," "rule of law and not of men"—these are weighted words addressed to the emotions. Such oratory usually appeals to Negroes and brings favorable responses. Therefore, partly because of Hoover's oratory, partly because the South revolted against the Democratic party in view of Governor Smith's religion, and partly because Mr. Hoover had emphasized his "Lily White" program, by which he won southern votes, he was elected. The South preferred a western, "Lily White" Republican to an eastern, Tammany, Negro-loving Democratic Catholic.

The campaign and election should have taught those who control the political parties one great lesson, at least, relative to the Negro's political loyalties; the Negro's vote was not to be responsive in the future only to Republicans' symbols, but more to the policies and personalities which offered the greatest returns in terms of deference and security. Since 1928 the Negro has come to regard political party labels as a means of identifying men, and not as determinants of what the party or the man stands for.

Governor Smith's record as chief executive of the Empire

78 Herbert Hoover, "Undermining Representative Government," an address delivered to the Joint Republican Organizations, Hartford, Conn., October 17, 1928.

State, his mastery of big business there, as well as his lowly origin, impressed Negroes. His refusal to take orders from Boss Murphy was a display of courage and independence of thought. In 1920, he opposed "Tammany" when it wanted to run William Randolph Hearst as Senator. In addition to those appealing qualities, he was vigorous in his opposition to the Ku Klux Klan, which avowedly hated Negroes, Catholics and foreigners. (Incidentally, Governor Smith was not the first Roman Catholic to be nominated for the Presidency. In 1872, Charles O'Conor of New York was so honored at a rump convention in Louisville, Kentucky, following the nomination of Horace Greeley by the regular organization.)[79]

His position in many ways contrasted with that of the Republican nominee, who was building a "Lily White" party in the South and promising little or nothing to the Negro. William MacDonald, Republican National Committeeman of Texas, summarized the situation in this manner: "Hoover carried the white South, but Smith the Negro."[80] This was probably a true observation because the Republicans were charged with being silent when the Reconstruction governments were overthrown; they did very little to prohibit the night ridings of the Ku Klux Klan and the intimidation, butchery and slaughter which accompanied the raids; they never raised their voice as an organized political group when the southern states were enacting the poll-tax laws and inserting into their respective constitutions "grandfather clauses" and property requirements as a condition of using the elective franchise. When educational clauses were inserted into the constitutions of several states and so administered that Negro Phi Beta Kappas and Ph.D's could not qualify, the Re-

79 Silas Bent, "Al Smith: Executive," *The Independent,* Independent Publications, Inc., New York, Volume CXX, Number 4078, 1928, 590-591.

80 *Fort Worth Eagle Eye,* Fort Worth, Texas, December 4, 1928.

publicans as a politically organized body said nothing.[81] These charges, although not true in every detail, indicate a break between the Negro and the Republican party. The Republicans' default from their early program toward the Negro was observed by some of the southern whites. Consider this expression by the great international scholar, Professor James Wilford Garner:

> Nearly twenty years have elapsed since Mississippi adopted a constitution which, in effect, took away from the Negro his political privileges, and although the party which has conferred political rights upon him has been in control of the national government during most of this period, no serious attempt has been made to interfere with the action of the state or to punish it by reducing its representation in Congress as the Fourteenth Amendment declares shall be done. Hardly a sincere and respectable protest against the disfranchisement of the Negro has yet been made by the Republican party and recent events would seem to justify the conclusion that it has virtually abandoned him as far as his political rights are concerned.[82]

A little later Professor Garner continues by declaring that:

> If the white people of the South exercise their power of control wisely and justly, it can be perpetuated to the end of time without protest or interference on the part of the country at large or indeed without serious opposition from the black race itself.[83]

81 *Opportunity*, October, 1927.

82 J. W. Garner, "New Politics for the South," *Annals of the American Academy of Political and Social Science, Philadelphia,* Volume XXXV, 1910, 174.

83 *Ibid.,* 461.

(William Pickens, a distinguished northern Negro, was to make a similar but much stronger statement in 1932. What was said by such men as Pickens and Garner cannot be lightly taken, for it is unusual for a northern Negro to share the political views of a southern white man, or vice versa, when they are dealing with the question of Negroes in politics.)

The successive platforms of the Republican party since 1915 show that the party for several years did not concern itself with anything relative to the Negro (1916-1928). In fact, when the convention met in Chicago on June 8, 1916, no direct reference was made to them.[84] In 1920, Warren G. Harding said, "We urge Congress to consider the most effective means to end lynching in this country which continues to be a terrible blot on our American civilization," but since several whites were lynched that year and the previous years, that cannot be said to be a pronouncement relative to the Negro.[85] President Coolidge in 1924 made a similar statement to that of Harding, but he also avoided the use of the term Negro. It was not until 1932 that a definite plank was put in the platform dealing with the welfare of the Negro as a notable group. The 1928 platform was as vague as those immediately preceding it. The platform of 1932 declared:

> For seventy years the Republican party has been the friend of the American Negro. Vindication of the rights of the Negro citizen to enjoy the full benefits of life, liberty and the pursuit of happiness is traditional in the Republican party and our party stands pledged to maintain equal opportunity and rights for our Negro

84 Kirk H. Porter, *National Party Platforms,* The Macmillan Company, New York, 1924, 395-402.

85 *Ibid.,* 461.

> citizens. We do not propose to depart from the tradition nor to alter the spirit or letter of that pledge.[86]

The platforms reflect the indifference of the party toward the Negro in that period. There is much speculation as to the causes for that, but speculation forms no essential part of this study, however interesting it might be. There are, however, two reasons for the Negro's complete reversal of attitude toward the "divinity" of the party; these do not fall in the category of speculation and should, therefore, be pointed out here. First, as we have seen, there was a tendency of the Republican party to forsake or ignore Negroes in the South. This, the Negro thought, was tantamount to endorsing the southern policy of "Lily Whitism" and other nefarious and undemocratic practices. Secondly, the party failed to keep its campaign pledges when it had the temerity to make them.

In summary, one sees that from the Civil War until 1932 nearly all of the Negroes were Republicans in politics. They could not have been otherwise, even if they had wanted to, for the Democrats did not want them, generally did nothing for them and *would not have them as members* of their party. The abandonment by the Republican party of its traditional position, the penetration into the North by a great number of energetic and intelligent Negroes since 1915 and the overtures made to them by the Democrats wooed the bulk of Negroes away from the Republican party, so that in 1932 they were somewhat in a doubtful state relative to party labels. The Negro, then, was divided largely along chronological lines. The old Negro was still Republican and emotionally tied to the party,[87] while the

86 *Ibid.*, 571.

87 See Appendix 3: Joseph D. Bibb, "Why I Am a Republican."

young Negro was dynamic and progressive and sought reason, security, positions, and deference as a condition of pledging his support to any party.[88] Before 1932 the Negro was a Republican without any modification; since 1932, as will be shown in the next chapter, when he is found remaining a Republican he requires all the modifications–Independent, Progressive, and Reactionary–that are in existence.

The Negro can thus say with Tennyson,

> Not once or twice, in our great Island Story
> The path of duty was the path of glory.

88 Appendix 4: Representative E. E. Green, "I Am a Republican," November 17, 1945. Attorney Green, a member of the Illinois Bar and Cook County Bar Association, was for four terms a member of the General Assembly of Illinois on the Republican ticket.

CHAPTER IV

The Negro and the Republican Party, 1932-1940

There is little reason, if any, to doubt that prior to 1932 the American Negroes as a group were generally loyal to the Republican party. The loyalty had its foundation, at least in part, in traditions and sentiments which extended back to the time when that party was organized in 1854. In the early days of the party's history one of the ablest Negro statesmen played at least a minor role and for that cause, if no other one existed, the Negroes thought the Republican party was the one with which they should align themselves.[1] Beginning about the middle of the nineteenth century and continuing without serious interruption until 1932 the political affiliation and political thought of the American Negroes was that of a single party—Republican—which had since that date (1854) consistently held sway over them. Indeed, prior to 1933 there had been little difference of

1 Frederick Douglass, *Life and Times of Frederick Douglass,* 358-66. See also Carter Woodson, editor, *Journal of Negro History,* Association for the Study of Negro Life and History, Washington, D.C., Volume XXIV, 1941, 413-84.

opinion among Negroes over what party to support although there are examples of differences among some of their leaders over what Republican candidate to support. With rare exceptions, they could be counted upon to follow loyally the party label in the state and national politics. The distinction between men and measures, issues and "isms," was not clear to them, and in many cases that distinction was ignored. Out of such a situation the Hoover Administration began in 1929.

The four years during which Mr. Hoover was President, 1929-1933, were in several ways heart-rending to the Negro as well as to the nation at large. The economic crisis which occurred shortly after the beginning of his term not only caused much suffering but it served to render Mr. Hoover increasingly unpopular. There were other occurrences, which will be discussed shortly, some of which can justly be attributed to Mr. Hoover while others were beyond his control. The occurrence which taxed the Negro's continued Republican loyalty was one that Mr. Hoover could not control and prevent. This was the depression which struck the country in 1929 and continued throughout his administration. Those who suffered as a consequence of the depression held Mr. Hoover responsible for it. That fact is shown by the frequent references to "Hoover's Depression." If the views of certain economists were taken for it, there would be little or no ground for making Mr. Hoover wholly responsible, for they had many years before propounded a theory which claimed that business disturbances, sometimes called crises or depressions, were predictable and occurred naturally at about seven-year intervals.[2] Under that theory the

2 S. J. Chapman, *Elementary Economics,* Longmans, Green and Company, New York, 1913, 45-97; Hugo Bilgram, *The Cause of Business Depression,* J. P. Lippincott Company, Philadelphia, 1913, 1-16; T. N. Carver, *Principles of Political Economy,* Ginn and Company, New York, 1919, 329-38.

year 1929 was overdue for a depression, since the previous one had occurred in the fall of 1921.

A discussion in an effort to demonstrate the value of that law has value in the immediate undertaking only insofar as it helps to fix or not fix responsibility on Mr. Hoover. If it can be shown, as some people claimed, that Mr. Hoover's grant of a moratorium to the debtor nations caused American businessmen to distrust generally the soundness of his policies and that as a consequence they would not expand domestically or make foreign investments, then Mr. Hoover was at least partly responsible for the depression. But if, on the contrary, depressions are the results of natural forces, even when they are predictable, and may not be controlled by finite man, then, Mr. Hoover was not responsible. There exists abundance of literature which supports both views, but for the purpose here it is significant that a depression occurred and as a result of it Negroes, like many other people, left the Republican party in large numbers.[3]

The intensity of the depression was increased in regard to the Negro because he had recently witnessed the greatest era of prosperity he had ever known in this country. In both the North and the South, many Negroes had purchased homes, made investments in life insurance, started small businesses, and in numerous other ways invested their savings and pledged their income from whatever source derived to meet their obligations.[4] When that depression struck the country it not only destroyed their savings in the banks and their investments, but it robbed them of an opportunity to continue to earn a livelihood by gainful employment; for, it is well known, the Negro is last to be

3 R. G. Tugwell, "Flaws in the Hoover Economic Plan," *Current History*, New York Times Company, New York, Volume XXXV, 1932, 525-31; also, in the same issue, Robert W. Morse, "President Hoover's Plan to Check the Depression," 263-64.

4 Monroe N. Work, *The Negro Yearbook, 1931-1932*, 118-38.

hired and the first to be discharged when depressions or crises occur in the industrial world. It was in part for those reasons they accepted the current slogan that this depression was caused by Mr. Hoover. They were led to believe that if Mr. Hoover were out of the White House, their opportunities to find security would be increased in business and industry. They cast their lot with that group in the campaign of 1932 which had adopted the slogan "Who but Hoover," not meaning that he was indispensable, but that anyone was more to be desired than he.[5]

In order to give the Negro's complaint against Mr. Hoover and the Republican party proper emphasis, the grievances of the nation as a whole are here indicated. It is generally acknowledged that the Negroes suffer from all of the common ailments which accompany a bad and deficient administration and in addition inherit others if for no reason other than the fact that they are Negroes.

Laborers, for example, claimed that his policies were responsible not only for their lack of employment opportunities, but also for the low wage scale in 1930-1932;[6] farmers were complaining about the high cost of implements and the low price of farm products.[7] Some business men saw in the enactment of the Hawley–Smoot Tariff law of 1930 a revival of the most objectionable features of the Payne-Aldrich Tariff law of 1908;[8] the war veterans saw in Mr. Hoover's treatment of those who had participated in the bonus march on the Capitol in July, 1932, a heartless dictator wedded only to the extreme con-

5 "Who But Hoover," editorial in *Collier's*, Crowell-Collier Publishing Company, New York, Volume LXXXVI, 1932, 12.

6 *Literary Digest*, Volume CVIII, October 7, 1932, 7-8.

7 "Hoover and the Wheat," editorial in *The Nation*, Volume CXXXIII, October 21, 1931, 431.

8 "The Revolt Against Hoover," editorial in *The Nation*, Volume CXXXI, July, 1930, 542.

servative doctrine.[9] Mr. Hoover's threat to veto the Relief Bill which would provide $2,125,000,000 of Federal money for the unemployed and needy people caused those who were in need to feel that their suffering was a matter of indifference to him.[10] They received some consolation, however, when on the next day, July 8, the House of Representatives passed the measure by a vote of 225 to 157.[11]

The above grievances constitute only a partial list of those that the general public had against Mr. Hoover. But as Mr. Hoover was the standard-bearer of the Republican party any public complaint against his policies was a complaint against his party. The Negro suffered from all of the above policies, and in addition, several specific ones. A few of the latter constitute such an important part of this book, since they were important factors in crystallizing thought against him, that a detailed treatment of them is given. The order in which those complaints appear here does not presume the order of their importance. Any arrangement would have some virtues as well as some faults, for the complaints were registered in different places by different people at different times often about different things.

On April 24, 1932, William Pickens, one of the most scholarly and one of the most courageous Negroes, assailed the Hoover Administration for its labor policy by which Negroes were excluded from the construction work at Boulder Dam. In a speech in Boulder, Colorado, he ridiculed white America for advertising the untruthful charge that "Negroes don't like to work," while at the same time compelling Negroes to fight for a job when the

9 A. G. Robinson and N. T. N. Robinson, editors, *Congressional Digest*, Washington, D.C., Volume X, 1932, 120-22.

10 *Chicago Daily Tribune, Chicago,* July 6, 1932, and July 7, 1932. (hereafter referred to as *Tribune*).

11 *Ibid.,* July 8, 1932.

government offers it. Dean Pickens' language will admit of no improvement:

> Work is the only thing which brought the Negroes to America. White people came seeking fortunes . . . expecting to exploit somebody. The Negro came only to work.

After Dean Pickens had carefully substantiated that assertion, he continued,

> He has worked faithfully for over three hundred years; he has nursed faithfully for three centuries white babies without kidnapping them—if the government could place black and white men in the same war trenches to fight and die in blood and muck supporting one another, that same government could put them on the same peace time job . . . Either colored workers will be put on this "dam" job or we will fight Herbert Hoover and all his henchmen for the next quarter century. We remembered an insult from Judge Parker for ten years; we will remember the Hoover crowd until they are all dead.[12]

That speech was given prominence by the Negro press. At least five of the leading papers gave a verbatim reproduction of it or commented upon it favorably.[13]

Because the press is one of the potent factors in molding public opinion it can be accepted as true that if the Negro's

12 *Chicago Bee,* April, 1932.

13 The writer consulted the following: *Black Dispatch*, Oklahoma City; *Kansas City Call,* Kansas City, Missouri; *Chicago Defender*, Chicago; *Pittsburgh Courier,* Pittsburgh; *Baltimore Afro-American,* Baltimore. The first three listed above contained the full text in their April 24, 1932, issues, while the latter two contained excerpts of it on the editorial page in their May 1, 1932, issues.

opinion was not then crystallized against Mr. Hoover, that speech went far toward effecting it. Negroes thought that at a time when they needed work most, and when the political party to which they had given unimpeachable loyalty for nearly three quarters of a century was in power, neither the government nor the party nor any responsible representative of that party should have initiated or tolerated a policy which was inimical to their best interests.[14] In the presidential campaign of that year much was written and spoken about the administration's segregation policy; the Boulder Dam incident was frequently cited as an example in proof.[15] One may conclude that the Negro's loyalty to Mr. Hoover and the Republican party suffered from the labor incident at Boulder Dam.

The Parker case was another cause for the Negro's revolt against Mr. Hoover and his party in the campaign of 1932. A few of the facts in that case might be mentioned here with profit, for it is only by having them fresh in mind that justification or condemnation of the Negroes' changed attitude toward Mr. Hoover and the Republican party can be made. During the early part of April, 1930, President Hoover sent the name of Judge John J. Parker of the United States Circuit Court of North Carolina to the Senate for confirmation as an Associate Justice of the United States Supreme Court. The nomination attracted the attention of the Negro people instantly, because of Judge Parker's expressed views relative to the Negro in 1920. In the same year, according to the *Greensboro Daily News* of April 19, 1920, he said,

> The Republican party of North Carolina has accepted the amendment in the spirit in which it was passed

14 *Pittsburgh Courier,* May 1, 1932.

15 *Amsterdam News,* October 4, 1932. Also, *St. Louis Argus,* St. Louis Argus Publishing Company, St. Louis, October 3, 1932.

> and the Negro has accepted it. I have attended every state convention since 1908 and I have never seen a Negro delegate in any convention that I attended. The Negro as a class does not desire to enter politics. The Republican party of North Carolina does not desire him to do so.

Then followed the statement that stirred the Negro's blood until it virtually boiled:

> We recognize the fact that he has not yet reached that stage in his development where he can share the burdens and responsibilities of government. This being true, and every intelligent man in North Carolina knows it is true, the participation of the Negroes in politics is a source of evil and danger to both races and is not desired by the wise men in either race or by the Republican party of North Carolina.[16]

That statement alone might have been ignored or covered over by the self-seeking Negro politicians, but some of his remarks in the campaign of 1920 were still echoing in their ears. In all of his speeches he announced that he never wanted any Negro to vote for him and that he would be happy if they would vote the Democratic ticket.[17]

When President Hoover nominated Judge Parker for the United States Supreme Court the Negro press and some of the white press were most articulate in condemning the act. Wil-

16 *Congressional Record,* Part VIII, 71st Congress, 2d Session, Government Printing Office, Washington, D.C., Volume LXXII, April 29—May 16, 1930, 8338 ff.

17 *Ibid.,* 8338.

liam Hard, a white newspaper man, described the situation as follows:

> First, the presidential campaign managers of 1928 discarded all efforts to please Negroes in favor of efforts to please southern whites.
>
> Second, the existing Republican administration has appointed virtually no Negroes to office.
>
> Third, the Negro division of the National Committee, under John R. Hawkins, has been closing down.
>
> Fourth, John J. Parker of North Carolina, accused of opposing Negro participation in politics, has been nominated to be a Justice of the Supreme Court of the United States.[18]

Mr. Hard agrees with the views generally held by Negroes that the Parker nomination would have been of minor importance if he or Hoover alone had not in previous actions prepared the Negro's mind for protest and revolt. That nomination was the match which set the proverbial dry hay on fire, or the straw which broke the proverbial camel's back.

A few of the press comments here will be not only revealing but helpful in developing the thesis that the nomination of Judge Parker turned many Negroes against Mr. Hoover and the Republican party.[19]

The *Boston Chronicle* declared:

> Mr. Hoover seems to have gone far afield to add insult to injury to the Negro, most loyal supporter of his party. In his zeal to compensate the white South for

18 *Ibid.*, 8339.

19 Except as otherwise indicated, these comments are found in *Congressional Record,* 71st Congress, 2d Session, Volume LXXII.

> its recent wholesale entry into Republican ranks, and his endeavor to hold them, the President has stopped at nothing short of contempt toward the Negro wing of the party.[20]

The *Chicago Defender* declared,

> If ever there was evidence of a president's disregard for opinion and welfare of a great number of his constituents, it is being shown in this particular case.[21]

The *Kansas City Call* commented,

> A Lincoln lost the senatorship from Illinois for principle's sake and became president. A Parker sought a governorship by subverting principle and will lose a Supreme Court judgeship.[22]

The *Black Dispatch* commented,

> Judge John J. Parker does not think the Negro has reached the stage in his development where he should participate in politics.
>
> Two great minds seem to be running in the same channel. The Negro does not think that Judge Parker has reached the place in his development where he should be allowed to sit on the Supreme Bench.[23]

These comments indicate how widespread the feeiing was against Judge Parker, and against President Hoover for nominating him. The Judiciary Committee of the Senate received thirty-six protests against Judge Parker and only three endorsements—

20 *Ibid.*, quoting, 8339.
21 Editorial, May 5, 1930, 1.
22 Editorial, May 4, 1930.
23 Editorial, May 5, 1930, 1 and 7.

one of those three was given by Mr. J. E. Shepard, Negro President of the North Carolina State College for Negroes, Durham, North Carolina. Mr. Shepard was popularly referred to by the opprobrious term "Uncle Tom"–one who has no convictions too sacred to surrender in the interest of appeasement. Another endorsement was given by M. K. Tyson who signed himself the Secretary of the National Association of Negro Tailors, Designers and Dressmakers. The third was given by Dr. Hubert F. Graft of Monroe, North Carolina. This last endorsement was sent to Senator Overman in the form of a letter and claimed that it carried with it the prayers of the colored people of Monroe (North Carolina) for the confirmation of Judge Parker.[24] The thirty-six who opposed Judge Parker represented all sections of the country and a variety of organizations, fraternal orders, religious bodies, college clubs, political groups and committees. Thus, the National Bar Association of Philadelphia, Pennsylvania, composed of over three hundred Negro attorneys asked Senator Joseph R. Grundy not only to vote against confirmation of Judge Parker, but also to use his influence with his colleagues to that end.[25]

Valuable as the above were in influencing the Senate's action, the most valuable opposition to Judge Parker's confirmation came from two other groups: organized labor, and the National Association for the Advancement of Colored People. The Negroes at that time seem to have caught the spirit of Patrick Henry when he stood in St. John's Church on March 22, 1775 and exclaimed:

> Besides, sir, we shall not fight our battle alone. There is a just God who presides over the destines of nations,

24 *Congressional Record,* Part VIII, 71st Congress, 2d Session, Volume LXXII, April 29 to May 16, 1930, 8340.

25 *Ibid.,* 8340.

> and who will raise up friends to fight our battles for us. The battle, sir, is not to the strong alone; it is to the vigilant, the active, the brave.[26]

Whether one can prove that the Negro shared Henry's feeling is not significant here; the fact is that a powerful group joined in the fight against Judge Parker which aided greatly in securing Judge Parker's defeat. That group was organized labor.

The position that organized labor took deserves more than passing notice here, for at that time there were very few Negro members in that group and Negroes were neither sought nor wanted in it, due in part to the fact that they had on a few occasions in the past been used as strikebreakers. Organized labor therefore did not enter the fight on humanitarian grounds, or especially because the Negro needed or requested its aid, but it entered the fight for another reason altogether. Just what was that reason?

Mr. Parker, while serving in the United States Circuit Court in North Carolina as its judge, had granted an injunction in a labor case which declared, in effect, that the so-called "yellow dog" contract was valid. A "yellow dog" contract was one under which men were employed on the condition that they would not join a labor union. Organized labor opposed that injunction because it was not only unfair to labor, but because it gave employers an opportunity to take advantage of job seekers who were in distress, and could force them to surrender their natural and constitutional rights. William Green, president of the American Federation of Labor, after having written President Hoover a letter urging withdrawal of Parker's nomination, pointed out that Negro opposition was politically significant

26 Kenneth Umbreit, "Men Who Shaped Our Tradition," *Founding Fathers,* Harper and Brothers, New York, 1941, (quoting:) 217-18.

due to the fact that the Negro vote in several of the northern states constituted the balance of power. He then asserted that when that vote was added to the vote of organized labor many thoughtful senators who were not anxious to lose their positions would vote to reject Judge Parker.[27] The Negroes, therefore, had a powerful ally in their fight even though it is doubtful whether the ally was motivated in its undertakings by considerations of the Negro's interests.

Just how did the Negro make himself effective in that undertaking, that is, the fight against the confirmation of Judge Parker by the Senate? That is a long, interesting story which centers largely around the activities of the National Association for the Advancement of Colored People.[28] A few of those facts lend themselves easily to a chronological arrangement.

First, the NAACP secured some of the judge's utterances from prominent people and from newspapers while he was campaigning for the governorship of North Carolina. These expressions, the Negroes said, were inimical to them as citizens and showed the dwarfed mentality of the nominee. (The statement refers to one mentioned previously.)

Secondly, the NAACP sent Judge Parker a telegram relative to the alleged remarks, which Judge Parker refused to answer. After having given him ample time to answer the telegram, and after no answer had been received, the NAACP then filed a formal protest with the Judiciary Committee of the Senate. The Senate, although Republican, the party which the Negro had loyally supported, and many of whose members were there because of the Negro's support, refused to consider the protest until all others who objected to his appointment had been heard.

27 *New York Evening Post,* D. S. Thackrey, publisher, New York City, May 4, 1930, 3.

28 Hereafter referred to as the NAACP.

Thirdly, the New York office of the NAACP contacted the local branches of the organization throughout the country and advised the local branches to use their influence with the people in the vicinity and have those flood Washington—the President, representatives and senators—with telephone calls, letters, telegrams, petitions, and personal visits, particularly those persons from the North and the border states, in an effort to block senatorial confirmation. They were told to remind their governmental representatives of the forthcoming election when their vote might be important. The senators' reaction to the barrage of communication was interesting: some thought that the protest would soon come to an end, while others expressed surprise; still others were bewildered at the Negro stepping out of his traditional role of meekness; still others were alarmed at the extent of the movement and began to wonder about its possible effects upon the next election.[29]

Fourthly, the NAACP asked President Hoover to withdraw the nomination of Judge Parker; in this way, Negro voters would escape the dilemma of either voting against the administration or voting against their best interests as a minority group. Some of the senators made a similar request to the White House, which the White House at first ignored.

Fifthly, the one Negro endorsement of Judge Parker was sent to the Judiciary Committee along with 188 affidavits from prominent Negroes tricked or bribed into making public utterance endorsing Judge Parker and stating that, when bribery failed, they were threatened.[30]

29 *Congressional Record,* Part VIII, Volume LXXVII, 8340-8342.

30 Walter White, "The Negro and the Supreme Court," *Harper's Monthly Magazine,* Harper and Brothers, New York, Volume CLXII, 1930, 238-40. Also, Homer L. Jack, *The History of the National Association for the Advancement of Colored People,* Meader Publishing Company, Boston, 1943, 106.

Sixthly, mass meetings were held in certain prominent cities, including Baltimore, Chicago, Detroit, Cleveland, Kansas City, Cincinnati, St. Louis, Los Angeles, and Philadelphia, and telegraph blanks were provided from which messages were sent to the respective senators. It was said that over two thousand were sent from Chicago to the senators from Illinois on the Sunday before the Senate's action was to be taken—many from churches, lodges, fraternities, sororities, and other organizations.[31]

Thus, the whole Negro electorate in the United States had been aroused in the Parker case. Dr. W. E. B. DuBois declared that

> It was a campaign conducted with a snap, determination, and intelligence never surpassed in Negro America and very seldom in white. It turned the languid, half-hearted protest of the American Federation of Labor into a formidable and triumphant protest. It fired the labored liberalism of the West into flame. It was ready to beat back the enemy at every turn . . . So in every twist and turn of the enemy the battle was pressed down to the last minute.[32]

When all of the material in opposition to Judge Parker is brought together, one finds three reasons for his rejection by the Senate. (The debates would take us too far afield were there undertaken here a discussion of them and what was said in them. For that reason the Negro Representative from Illinois, Oscar DePriest, has been left out of this story, even though he used every influence at his command to prevent Judge Parker's confirmation.)

31 *Harper's Monthly Magazine,* Volume CLXII, 239.
32 *The Crisis,* June, 1930.

First and foremost was his attitude toward the Negro, second his attitude toward organized labor, and last but still quite important the belief and the fear on the part of some southerners that Parker's nomination was an effort by the Republicans to add North Carolina permanently to the Republican fold.[33]

It was by anybody's measurement one of the greatest political demonstrations on the part of the Negro since the Civil War, or at least since the end of the Reconstruction period.[34] The effect of that political demonstration was felt for some time thereafter. For example, one Kansas Senator seeking re-election the summer of 1930 in a district predominantly Negro polled only 27 per cent of the votes where normally the Republicans polled 75 per cent.[35] In Ohio one finds a similar situation when Senator R. C. McCulloch was campaigning for re-election after he had filled the unexpired term of Senator Theodore E. Burton. The Negro voters of the state without regard to political affiliation and other circumstances united against Senator McCulloch because of his stand in the Parker case.[36]

The importance of the Parker case from the Negro's point of view lay in the fact that the Negro had come to believe that in the Federal Supreme Court he stood his best chance of receiving justice. That court had rendered several decisions that had far-reaching effect on his constitutional right.[37] It was considered his last resort when everything else had gone against him. Since Judge Parker by sins of commission—the campaign

33 Discussion among Senators Stephens, Ashurst, and Caraway, *Congressional Record,* Part VIII, Volume LXXVII, 8343-44.

34 *The Crisis,* September, 1929, 63.

35 *Kansas City Call,* July 9, 1930.

36 *Cleveland Plain Dealer,* July 8, 1930.

37 Several of those cases are discussed by Monroe N. Work, *The Negro Yearbook,* volumes for the years 1916-40, inclusive; and several of the more recent cases are discussed by Florence Murray, *The Negro Handbook,* 1944, 30-42.

speeches in 1920—and the sin of omission—refusal to reply to the letters, telegrams and telephone calls directed to him by the NAACP—was unfit for the bench, the Negroes assumed it as their responsibility to prevent, if possible, his confirmation. How well they succeeded is told by his overwhelming rejection by the Senate in 1930.

Another specific complaint which the Negro had against President Hoover and the Republican party was caused by Mr. Hoover's attitude and policies toward the so-called "Lily White" movement. That movement did not begin with Mr. Hoover. The term is thought to have been coined in Texas in 1888 by the Negro Republican leader, Norris Wright Cuney.[38] There seems to have been a fight between the Negro and white Republicans who were struggling for the control of a convention, after which the term was applied to designate the white Republicans in that state and the rest of the southern states. Their objective was to purge the Republican party of the South of Negro leadership, Negro control, and a share in the spoils of victory. The argument was that the white South should divide between the major parties, that the time had come for many southerners to be converted to Republicanism, but that the southern white men would not join a Republican party which tolerated Negroes.

Prior to 1930 "Lily White" groups had functioned in every southern state except West Virginia and Kentucky, and had sometimes been sufficiently strong to give considerable trouble to Negro "regulars."[39] Their object was, ostensibly, to attract white men into the party, and in order to accomplish that they

38 Gunnar Myrdal, *An American Dilemma,* Harper and Brothers, New York, Volume I, 478-79.

39 *New York Times,* July 17, 1928.

felt obliged to discourage Negro voters, dispose of Negro committeemen and convention delegates, and thus "clean up the party." For example, in 1892 in the state of Texas, a group of white Republicans revolted from the regular organization, held a convention of its own and sent a contesting delegation to the Republican National Convention. The white delegation was for McKinley; while the Negro delegation was for either Allison or Reed. Cuney and his friends were turned down for the McKinley whites.[40] The situation became so tense between the "Lily White" faction and the so-called "Black and Tan" faction that at least in one state an injunction was sought to prevent Negroes from holding a state convention—Florida.[41]

In the entire political history of Virginia there had been only two occasions prior to 1930 in which a real contest occurred in the state's election sufficient to draw in the Negro vote. The first was in 1921 when the "Lily Whites" openly entered the field, and the second was in 1929 when the "Hoovercrats" and the regular Democrats split and sent separate nominees to the November polls.[42] In 1921 Henry W. Anderson had secured control of the "Lily White" faction of the Republican State Convention, and instantly, a Negro ticket was put in the field. It is thought by some observers that this was not wholly a matter of rebuking the Anderson faction nor even preparation of a show of strength to impress the national party organization, but that it was done after conferences with the white party officials—the object being to provide an outlet for Negro indignation without compromising the Democratic ticket by a sudden adherence to Negro voters.[43] In the election which followed,

40 M. C. Hare, *Norris Wright Cuney,* Associated Publishers, Washington, D.C., 1913, 92.

41 *New York Times,* December 30, 1919.

42 *Ibid.,* July 17, 1928.

43 *Ibid.,* August 6, 1928.

Trinkle's ticket won, Anderson ran second, while Mitchell, the Negro aspirant for the governorship, ran third.[44] There was some belief that Mitchell and his friends had been used to draw Negroes from the growing Republican opposition.[45]

In 1928 a "Lily White" organization rivaling the traditional Negro and regular bodies had sprung up in nearly every southern state except West Virginia and Kentucky. The events surrounding the nomination and election of Herbert Hoover gave the movement additional prominence, for in view of the confusion into which the South had been thrown by the nomination of the wet, Catholic, "Tammany" Smith the time seemed ripe for a genuine Republican campaign in the South. Mr. Hoover seems to have hoped that by working through the "Lily White" organizations and by use of underground party politics he would finally merge the South into an anti-Smith camp.[46]

As the newspaper accounts are read of the Republican organization for 1928, the impression is obtained that the tide in that organization was running against the "Black and Tan" regulars. Ben Davis, colored National Committeeman from Georgia, was given money for pre-convention expenses from a regular party source, yet he testified to his uneasiness over the officious activities of a white man, Clark Greer, who seemed to have been in charge for Mr. Hoover.[47] After Mr. Hoover's election his suspicion was borne out when Mr. Hoover discharged him (Ben Davis) from the Republican Council.[48] Perry W.

44 *World Almanac*, published by the *New York World*, New York, 1928.

45 That charge was heard frequently in Virginia in 1928, but the writer found no documents to support it; hence, it seems to be historical gossip.

46 *New York Times*, November 20, 1928. That editorial declared that Mr. Hoover did not intend to make a clean sweep of the "Black and Tan" Republicanism in the convention, but got appreciable support from it.

47 *Ibid.*, May 20, 1928.

48 *Ibid.*, November 20, 1928.

Howard, another Negro "regular" who at that time was Assistant United States Attorney General and National Committeeman from Mississippi, was permitted to bring a Hoover delegation to the convention, but had "to walk in fear" of a "Lily White" organization which he claimed had been encouraged by Mr. Hoover at the time of the flood relief work of 1927.[49] During the campaign the work in Mississippi for the election of Mr. Hoover for president was in charge of the "Lily White" organization under Lamont Rowland, a recent accession to the party.

At the convention Walter Cohen, the Negro leader from Louisiana, was seated, but the other eleven delegates, all "Lily White" Hoover men, were led by the "Lily White" Emil Kuntz.[50] Henry W. Greager was in charge of a "Lily White" delegation from Texas and at that convention (1928) was seated over the protest of the Negro National Committeeman, "Goose Neck" Bill McDonald, and his one white Republican Representative, Wurzback, who owed his seat to the Negro voters of San Antonio.[51]

Mr. Hoover was nominated and elected, largely because he had been successful in building up a "Lily White" organization in the South and because he was able to play upon the emotions of the people there in such a way as to turn them against his "wet, Catholic, Tammany" dominated rival, as Lamont Rowland of Mississippi puts it.[52] After Mr. Hoover had taken office as President of the United States he made other utterances that had not clarified his position and policies relative to Negro consideration and deference but re-emphasized his determination

49 *Ibid.*, May 30, 1928. Also June 7, 1928.

50 *Ibid.*, June 6 and 7, 1928.

51 *Ibid.*, June 6, 1928.

52 *Corinthian*, Klyce and Bishop, editors and publishers, Corinth, Mississippi, November 14, 1928. A clipping from the above paper was sent to the writer in March, 1933, by Lamont Rowland.

to "play ball" with the "Lily White" factions of the Republican party.

"Successive presidents have long wished to build up a Republican party in the South such as would commend itself to the citizens of those states," he declared. (The implication here is that he did not regard the Negro as a citizen.) Then he commended the "Lily White" state committees in Virginia, North Carolina, Alabama, Arkansas, Louisiana, Texas, and Florida; but said he,

> In South Carolina, Georgia, and Mississippi, recent exposure of abuses in the sale of patronage obviously render it impossible for the old organization . . . to command the confidence of the administration. . . . The duty of reorganization rests with the people of those states, and all efforts to that end will receive the hearty cooperation of the administration. . . . If these three states are unable to initiate such an organization . . . the different federal departments will be compelled to adopt other measures to secure advice as to the selection of federal employees.[53]

This is by far the boldest and most expansive public gesture toward the "Lily Whites" made by a responsible Republican spokesman to be found. It let the Negroes know anew that the Hoover administration did not want them and furthermore was not going to do anything politically new for them. The situation then confronting the Negro in the South was this: The Republican party, was indifferent toward him; the administration in Washington had repudiated him; and the Democrats as a whole would not have him.

53 *New York Times,* March 27, 1929.

By the time the meeting of the National Convention approached in July, 1932, the Negro press had pointed out so often to the Negro what Mr. Hoover's policies had been that Mr. Hoover did not have the best wishes of many of the Negro leaders.[54] The contests between the Mississippi "Lily Whites" and "Black and Tan" factions over which should be seated in Chicago was said to have cost the state twelve ballots.[55] In that state the white Republicans were controlled by Lamont Rowland, a wealthy lumber man of Corinth, Mississippi, while the "Black and Tans" were controlled by an eminent Negro physician, S. D. Redmond, assisted by Attorney Perry W. Howard and Mary C. Booze. J. C. Tyler, secretary of the State's Central Committee of the "Lily White" group, claimed that he had received the official call from the national headquarters. What took place at the convention seems to indicate the correctness of Mr. Tyler's claim, for only a few Negro delegates were seated and those of S. D. Redmond were rejected.[56]

There was a similar fight over the Georgia Republican delegates resulting in only two of the sixteen Negroes which Georgia sent to the Convention being seated—Benjamin Davis, former National Committeeman of the state, and Dr. W. H. Harris. Clent W. Hagar, white, was given the place formerly held by Captain A. T. Walden in the 1928 convention.[57] Opposition to the Negro in the party was led by a woman, Mrs. George S. William, Republican National Committeewoman of that state.

In Tennessee Robert Church had a fight with the "Lily Whites." C. A. Bruce, a wealthy lumberman who had once been a candidate for governor on the Republican ticket, headed the "Lily White" group. Robert Church headed the "Black and

54 *Chicago Bee,* May 1, 1932.
55 *Ibid.*
56 *Ibid.,* July 26, 1932.
57 *Ibid.,* April 17, 1932.

Tan" group. Their skirmish started when Bruce attempted to make a speech before a stormy convention in Memphis, at which time Church's supporters jeered him down. Bruce then declared that he was out for Church's scalp, and would seek the recognition of his faction at Chicago. Bruce pointed out that his faction "although known as the 'Lily White' group had some Negroes in it." Seven of his twenty delegates were Negroes.[58]

Walter Cohen of Louisiana and William McDonald of Texas, both of whom had dominated Republican politics in their states, were personally seated; but the delegations which they led were either not seated at all or they were given only one half-vote. The 1932 convention marked the first time that there had been such a fight over the seating of Negro delegates since 1912, and the Hoover attitude and effort to build up a "Lily White" party in the South was thought to have been responsible for it. In consequence of that belief, the Negro could not and did not support him unitedly in the campaign which followed. A close student of political affairs has made an analysis of the votes which the political parties polled for 1932. He found that the Negro clergymen and lawyers were predominantly Republicans in 1932; but the physicians, housewives, students, laborers, and domestic workers showed a preference for the Democratic candidate.[59] Since the latter group contained the bulk of the Negroes of voting age, that analysis leads to the conclusion that the Negro did not give Mr. Hoover his loyal support in 1932 as he had formerly given it to the Republican party.

A very brief statement should be made relative to another complaint which the Negroes had against the "Hoovercrats," for

58 *Ibid.*, ANP releases.

59 *Opportunity, Journal of Negro Life,* National Urban League, New York, May, 1932, 141 (hereafter referred to as *Opportunity*).

it was something that aroused much interest among the Negroes at the time. It was the segregation of the Gold Star Mothers when they planned to visit the graves of their sons who had fallen in France in World War I. Many outstanding Negro women refused the trip because of the humiliating way that it was offered to them. There were many protests filed with the Secretary of War, Patrick J. Hurley, about the affair.[60] Secretary Hurley did not deny that the plan was to segregate the Gold Star Mothers, but he tried to assure the Negroes that their accommodations would be in every respect the same as those of the whites. Negroes knew this assertion was untrue for at that very time the white women frequented the best hotels in New York, while the Negro women had to resort to the cheap boarding houses.[61] A careful student of race relations declared that four hundred and fifty Negro women had planned to make the trip, but, because of the Hoover policy of providing separate, unequal accommodations, only fifty-eight made it.[62] After several protests had been filed with Secretary Hurley he compromised somewhat in his stand and declared that so far as he was concerned the women of both races could make the trip together, provided such agreement could be reached among the women themselves.[63] He knew that to be impossible due to the southern attitude.

The folly of the policy is emphasized when it is set over against the eloquent plea contained in an editorial of the *Boston Post* under the title, "Be Fair to the Mothers." The editor declared:

60 *New York Times,* July 11, 1930, 10. Also, *The Crisis,* July, 1930.

61 Walter White, Executive Secretary, National Association for the Advancement of Colored People, in *The Crisis,* July, 1930.

62 *Ibid.,* July, 1930.

63 *New York Times,* July 11, 1930, 10.

> Serious difficulties have arisen in connection with the tours of the Gold Star Mothers. . . . Already nearly a third of the mothers assigned to the initial pilgrimage have withdrawn. Other cancellations are coming in daily.[64]

After this, the editor made a plea for the government to give those who could not make the trip the actual cost of the trip in cash. That would amount to about $850; but one searches in vain for an expression from Mr. Hoover supporting the idea, even though it was strongly urged upon him by the NAACP through its Executive Secretary, Walter White.[65]

The conclusion to which these incidents lead is that the Republican party under Mr. Hoover had through the Parker case, the "Lily White" policy and the Gold Star Mothers' affair alienated the Negro's loyalty to the party. Those grievances in addition to the grievances held by the general public, which held Mr. Hoover somewhat responsible for the business crash which began in 1929, had not only made the Negro exclaim in 1932 "Who but Hoover" but also made the nation at large join in the song. The election return is eloquent proof.

It would be missing the point to see the Negro bolting the Republican party fully in the 1932 election or to think that he became aware, for the first time, of Republican insincerity and indifference during the Hoover administration. The truth of the matter is that certain Negroes had been cognizant of such a tendency since 1876 when it was thought that the Republicans made a deal with the South during the Hayes-Tilden deadlock whereby Hayes, the Republican candidate, was to be

64 Richard Grozier, editor, *Boston Post,* Post Publishing Company, Boston, April 7, 1930.

65 *The Crisis,* July, 1930.

made President, in return for which Mr. Hayes was to take the United States Army out of the South and leave the Negroes in the hands of their former slave masters.[66] Nearly every anti-Negro policy found in any of the former Republican administrations was used by Mr. Hoover while he was in the White House. He neither showed deference to the Negro nor gave any unique positions to him.

Such indifference seemed to increase the political friction between the Negro and the white of the South as was evidenced by the formation of the "Loyal League" in Georgia. That League was a sort of bureau of the radical Republican party whose chief object was to control the Negro vote.[67] The League did not oppose use of the franchise if it would aid in electing the kind of officers the whites had had since the overthrow of the Reconstruction government. All students of political science know that Mr. Hoover was badly beaten in the election of 1932 by Franklin Delano Roosevelt. Since 1933 the Republicans have tried to recapture the Negro vote in a variety of ways, but their vitriolic expressions, their skill in the manipulation of propaganda symbols, their emotional pleas, and their expenditures of large sums left Mr. Landon in 1936 and Mr. Willkie in 1940 in no better circumstance with the Negro than Mr. Hoover was in November, 1932.

The Republicans blamed the New Deal relief, which was partly correct, for their losing the Negro vote, but they are equally at fault, for they did nothing to prevent it. Earl Brown, writing for *Opportunity* in December, 1936, estimates that over 2,000,000 Negroes voted in the election of that year. He asserts:

66 Editorial, *Chicago Bee,* October 1, 1944. See also John R. Lynch, *The Facts of Reconstruction,* 156-61.

67 Robert F. Carson, "The Loyal League in Georgia," *Georgia Historical Quarterly,* Savannah, Volume XX, Number I, March, 1936, 125-53.

> That was the first time since the Reconstruction Amendments that the majority of Negroes voted for a Democratic president. That situation made the race an integral part of both major parties and increased them in political stature and importance.[68]

He continued by pointing out four additional things this election implied or achieved. First, the increased political activity among Negroes in the South was the most important political movement for them and for the poor whites. The latter saw that because the Negroes were disfranchised, they were too. Secondly, more Negroes voted in the South than at any time since Reconstruction. In Durham, North Carolina, over 4,000 voted as contrasted with about 500 in previous national elections. Thirdly, there was little opposition to the Negroes voting in many places; the press carried no releases about the whites intimidating the Negroes because some of them (Negroes) went to the polls. Fourthly, he claimed that the New Deal had abolished sectionalism to a greater extent than any other force in history.[69]

Between 1932 and 1940 the nation had seen the Negroes swing far to the left, not only by electing liberal-minded white men as Democrats to offices in the nation's capital, but it had also seen them elect a politically unknown Negro, Arthur Mitchell, who at the time had been in the district from which he was elected for less than six years. This election is all the more significant because he was elected over the militant Republican Negro Congressman, Oscar DePriest. Mitchell used as a slogan "Forward with Roosevelt" while Oscar DePriest, the Republican, constantly appealed to the people to give him support because,

68 *Opportunity*, Volume XIV, Number 12, 359-61.
69 *Ibid.*, 360.

first, he was a Republican, and, secondly, because of his record. In 1936 we find that in the United States as a whole, sixteen Negroes were elected to the state legislatures—eleven Democrats and five Republicans. The state of Pennsylvania led with electing five from the city of Philadelphia—one being Reverend Marshall Shepard who later offered prayer in the Democratic Convention meeting at Philadelphia in July, 1940. His recognition caused some of the southern whites to bolt their party, for example, Senator Edward (Cotton Ed) Smith of South Carolina.[70] The significant thing about that election is that the Negro showed a change in political thought that was far-reaching in that he not only left the Republican party in national politics but was seeking positions in state and local government on the Democratic ticket.

The Landon campaign was supported very mildly even by the Negro Republicans. In fact, some of the best Negro political minds which had formerly been Republican fought him ferociously. For example, the learned Kelly Miller wrote a series of articles for the ANP in which he urged the Negroes to support President Roosevelt.[71] Bishop R. R. Wright of the African Methodist Episcopal Church not only wrote articles for the ANP but organized a committee, the purpose of which was to fight Landon and the Republicans.[72] How well they succeeded is seen in the election returns—Landon carried only two states and neither of those has a Negro population large enough to have swung the election for him even had all Negro residents supported the Republican candidate.

Mr. Wendell Willkie, the Republican standard-bearer in the

70 For the states from which Negroes were elected, other data relative to the votes received, the opposing candidates, etc., see the *Chicago Bee,* November 15, 1936.

71 *Ibid.,* October 11, 1936, and all of the November, 1936, issues.

72 *Ibid.,* November 3, 1936.

1940 campaign, was given far more support by Negroes than Mr. Landon had received four years earlier. The Negro press seemed less critical of him than of Mr. Landon, even though there was no outstanding Negro paper which unconditionally supported his candidacy.[73] Some of the minor Negro papers were found supporting both of the candidates.[74]

The Republican situation as far as the Negro was concerned had made the Negro conscious of the party's lack of divinity. By 1940, he had come to look upon political parties somewhat as though they were two bottles which still retained on them their labels after the contents had been emptied. It was then (1940) a man-measure matter with the Negro, not an emotional attachment to a party label.

73 The most popular Negro papers are:*Pittsburgh Courier, Chicago Defender, The Afro-American, Kansas City Call,* and *Amsterdam News.* Issues for October and November of those papers were consulted; although they did not fight Mr. Willkie, they did not give open support to him.

74 *Chicago Bee, St. Louis Argus,* and *Black Dispatch* were for Roosevelt; *New York Age* and *Cleveland Plain Dealer* supported Willkie. See October and November, 1940, issues.

CHAPTER V

The Negro and the Democratic Party

In 1940 the population of continental United States was 131,669,275; of that number Negroes constituted 12,865,518, or 9.7 per cent.[1] In any group of such proportions it would be most unusual if there were no instances of some of the group who had never been associated with other organizations if both its members and the other organizations had had a fairly long history. Research reveals that in certain localities Negroes had been affiliated with the Democratic party for many years prior to 1932—proof that exclusion of the black man from participation in activities of the party was not a universal practice.[2] In Chapters III and IV it was established that prior to 1932 most of the Negroes in the United States were Republicans, and had been

1 Florence Murray, *The Negro Yearbook,* 1944, 14-15; also, *World Almanac,* 1945, 460 and 491.

2 Claude McKay, *Harlem: Negro Metropolis,* E. P. Dutton and Company, New York, 1940, Chapters 2-4.

Republicans since the time the party was organized. Indeed, there had been instances, beginning shortly after the emancipation, of some Negroes aligning themselves with the Democratic party. There had been some advocacy for them to desert the Republican party, advocacy which began shortly after emancipation. Such advocacy has increased in intensity and quantity since the turn of the century. This affiliation with the Democratic party in recent years can be considered a new alignment only in the sense of its having a new welcome by a larger number of Democrats. Democrats since the campaign of 1932 have appealed for Negro support, and have attracted a large number of new recruits, most of whom were formerly Republicans. Prior to 1932 there were a few instances of Negroes supporting the Democratic ticket.

For example, as early as 1868 the Democratic party in New York City secured John A. Nail, a Negro saloon keeper and one of the leading citizens of his community, to set up a Negro Democratic club in that city. He directed its activities in the interest of Democrats until he retired to private life in 1900. He was succeeded by Ferdinand Q. Martin, who regularly campaigned for election of Democratic candidates until 1920 when the club was put in charge of the skillful and eloquent Mrs. Bessye Bearden.[3] During the long history of the club's existence, Negroes were abundantly rewarded in many ways.

There are many examples of Negroes becoming increasingly aware of the wisdom of aligning themselves with more than one political party. For example, in 1905 the Niagara movement was initiated by a group of prominent Negro educators and influential citizens. Among the many things which they did were: to condemn in strong language the Republican party for

3 *Ibid.*, 124-31.

having obtained Negro support under false pretenses; to recommend a change, or at least a modification, in the future alignment of the Negro; and to dedicate themselves to a program of political uplift and enlightenment for that race.[4]

In 1906, the popular and influential *New York Age,* a Negro weekly, gave its support to the same thesis when its courageous editorial declared:

> When the Negro leaders learn how to utilize the fact that the Democratic party (in the North at any rate) would be glad to get the Negro vote and that the Republican party would be aghast at losing it, they will no longer have reason to complain of political neglect.[5]

In some circles the question is still debated whether newspapers make public opinion or whether they reflect it. Such a debate may have value in arriving at certain technical decisions relative to priority. In the matter under consideration, however, it is sufficient to know there was a prominent Negro leader who, while editor of a popular Negro weekly, exhibited sufficient courage, foresight and wisdom to warn his people of the folly of affiliating themselves with only one political party.

A similar position to that expressed by the *New York Age* was taken in 1908 by Dr. Horace Blumstead (white), president of Atlanta University, a Negro school, when he urged the Negro to desert the Republican party and support a new third party

4 *The Public,* The Public Publishing Company, Chicago 1905, Volume VIII, 257-265; Volume XII, 639. Some of the prominent personalities in attendance were W. E. B. DuBois, Kelly Miller, William M. Trotter, J. H. Summers, W. C. Payne, and T. H. A. Moore.

5 *Ibid.,* 1906, Volume VIII, 221, quoting *New York Age.*

as a means of preventing his extinction as a political factor. He declared:

> For years the Republican party has been showing a diminishing disposition to do anything for the protection of the Negro and an increasing acquiescence in the placing of liabilities upon him by unfriendly hands. The case has been aggravated by the fact that the Negro has not asked for special legislation in his interest as for a race that wanted to be petted and coddled, but simply for the protection of his ordinary rights of citizenship as conferred upon him by law, and especially by the war amendments to the United States Constitution which were secured by the Republican party.[6]

Again in October, 1908, some Negroes of Brooklyn, New York, effected an organization which had as one of its objectives freeing their race from representation by white Republicans, the few Negroes who were selfishly seeking office and the few officeholders attentive only to their own interests. The editor of *The Public* commented upon the movement as follows:

> If that organization was made in good faith it deserves encouragement. It is natural enough for Negroes in gratitude for its having released them from slavery to vote for the Republican party long after it has ceased to represent the least anti-slavery spirit. . . . The persistency of the Negro in herding together in politics, not for their race but for conscienceless exploiters of both races, has been their greatest weakness.[7]

6 *The Independent,* The Independent Publishing Company, New York, Volume LXXIV, 1908, 1322-34.

7 *The Public,* Volume IX, October 27, 1908, 551-52.

Such comments and excerpts, representing as they do a variety of opinions, foreshadow the Negroes' affiliation with the Democratic party since 1932. Consequently it was not solely the result of the personality, the program and the pull of F. D. Roosevelt and the New Deal, nor was it the result of Herbert Hoover and the Republicans. Both helped to hasten it, but it was, in part at least, due to serious thought on the part of some of the Negro leaders. Such thought, in some instances, goes back to the period of Reconstruction or shortly after the Civil War.

The history of the United States is replete with examples of the manner in which a crisis brings people's attention to a focal point relative to far-reaching reforms and procedures. The mere suggestion of the crisis itself will recall to the student of American history the reforms which have followed crisis. Thus, the Revolutionary War, the formation of the Constitution, the Revolution of 1800, the calamity of 1819, the Civil War, the panic of 1873, the business failures of 1893, the Bull Moose upsurge of 1912, the World War of 1917-1918, and the severe economic crisis beginning in 1929—all of these broke in upon the ordinary routine of life and were accompanied by a series of modifications in both thought and action.

When all has gone well, and when as former Senator Huey P. Long of Louisiana said "every man a king" becomes a reality, or, as Dr. F. E. Townsend had it, "ham and eggs for breakfast for every man," there is need for little thought beyond the routine. A crisis tends to awaken people out of their slumber; they are inclined not only to wonder how they got into the difficulty but also to try to devise schemes for getting out. In nearly every American crisis there has been an upturn of liberal ideas and a breaking with some traditions. If we go back no further than the economic crisis of 1893 we find that the Populist party gave its support to such a contention by its attack upon "accumulated wealth." An examination of its platform of 1893 reveals a number of planks so far-reaching in popular appeal that the Hanna, the Lodge, and the McKinley groups had to recede from their conservative positions.[8] A crisis, therefore, affects the political thought and behavior of most people: rich, poor, colored, white, the majority and the minority.

The economic crisis which occurred in 1929 brought the Negro into the Democratic fold as much as any single event. Indeed, if Hoover had been president during a period of prosperity, his indifference toward the Negro, his "Lily White" policy, the Parker nomination, and the Gold Star Mothers' controversy would probably have been ignored and to some extent forgotten. This combination of incidents was more than the Negroes or whites could stand; hence in 1932 there was a landslide for Franklin D. Roosevelt, who polled 472 electoral votes to Hoover's 59.[9]

A discussion of the Negro in the National Democratic Convention would have little, if any, merit in this study. Not until the convention of 1936 were there any Negro delegates; there were thirty at that convention. Prior to this the Democrats did not want the Negroes and the Negroes in large numbers did not seek membership with the Democratic party. But, after the Roosevelt landslide of 1932, the picture began to change; there was a kind of feeling of mutual dependence upon each other, the Democrats depending upon the Negroes' vote because in many places Negroes constituted the balance of power in a closely contested election, and the Negro depending upon the Democrats because the Democrats were in power and had control of much of the employment and nearly all of the relief.

8 Kirk H. Porter, *National Party Platforms,* The Macmillan Company, New York, 1924, 196-200, 201-6.

9 *World Almanac,* 1933, 737.

So the Negro vote in certain pivotal states would constitute a kind of assurance for a Democratic victory if the election there was close; for the Negro to declare himself to be a Democrat or to register as a Democrat was a kind of assurance of continuing to receive relief aid or a relief job. In Chicago, for example, the ward committeeman of the Fourth Ward had a list of jobs printed that would be available after the election. These jobs could be obtained only upon the recommendation of the precinct captains.[10] It is obvious that the precinct captains would designate and recommend only party adherents. Therefore, relief and employment were means of recruiting large numbers of Negroes into the Democratic fold.

Another factor was the personality and the philosophy of the President. A discussion of his personality would lead into the field of psychology, but the President's political philosophy cannot be ignored. He did not take the position that the strength of the country was to be found solely in the fighting forces; but his position was "the strength of this country is to be found somewhat in the intelligence, the freedom, and the health of the people."[11] The slogans "The New Deal" and "No Forgotten Man" especially appealed to the Negro, for many of them knew that the race had been in need of a new deal in politics in the United States since the withdrawal of the Federal troops from the South shortly after the Reconstruction period.[12] Indeed, many Negroes were cognizant of the fact that in things political and social, Republican presidents and administrations had conveniently and consistently forgotten them since 1908.

10 Harold F. Gosnell, *Negro Politicians*, University of Chicago Press, Chicago, 1935, 134.

11 F. D. Roosevelt, *Looking Forward,* The John Day Company, New York, 1933, 200-228. Also, *On Our Way*, same author and publisher, 1943, 223-230.

12 John R. Lynch, *The Facts of Reconstruction,* 156-60.

Negroes asked "where are the spoils of victory, and where is the trust, the honor and the deference which the candidate promised?" The slogans "New Deal" and "No Forgotten Man" coming as they did from an administration which was keeping its promises by providing work and increasing relief allotments made a very strong impression on Negroes.

Slogans without positive, concrete acts would have little effect, for the life of a nation or of a race cannot forever be stimulated solely by slogans. Indeed, hungry humanity requires deeds, actions and concrete proof for such assertions as a "New Deal" or "No Forgoten Man." Accordingly, President Roosevelt launched his great humanitarian program under a series of alphabetical designations, some of which were AAA, CCC, HOLC, NYA, PWA, and WPA. These dealt with nearly every phase of human welfare. Such a program, could it have been free from spoils, as practiced by some of the politicians, would have, nevertheless, brought into the Democratic party a large number of new Negro recruits, for by the middle of 1934, President Roosevelt had given Negroes more favorable consideration by appointing members of that race to administrative positions than had ever been given by any other president.[13] Most of those positions had to do with the administration of the welfare agencies; it was by means of those agencies that President Roosevelt intended to relieve the country from the distress of the depression and restore public confidence.[14] How well he succeeded is indicated by his "purge" from the party of certain individuals who opposed his program and by the election returns in 1936. In 1932, Roosevelt's popular vote was 7,060,016 more than Hoover's (Roosevelt–22,821,857; Hoover–15,761,841), while he received 472 of the electoral votes to Hoover's 59. In

13 Florence Murray, *The Negro Handbook,* 155-58.

14 F. D. Roosevelt, *Looking Forward,* 157-93.

1936, however, President Roosevelt polled 27,476,673; while Governor Landon polled 16,679,583, that is, Roosevelt had 10,797,090 more popular votes and 523 electoral votes out of a total of 531.[15] The significance expressed and implied by these statistics lies in the fact that Mr. Roosevelt was more popular after his first term than before.

It would be a grave error to assume that President Roosevelt kept all of the planks in the Democratic platform or all of his pre-election promises. Presently it will be shown that this was not the case. "Platforms are made for candidates to stand on before elected and to lie on after election" is a witticism which expresses with accuracy and aptness the American political creed. There has not been a president from Washington to Roosevelt who has not been accused by his political adversaries of ignoring or disregarding or discarding his pre-election promises. In fact, it is no reflection upon the honor and integrity of a president if he is forced to do so in the light of changing conditions. Any efficient administration should be actuated not entirely by campaign pledges but by the exigency of the situation. For example, Abraham Lincoln was elected on a platform which bound him not to interfere with the institution of slavery in states where it already existed, yet by an autocratic assumption of power he issued the Emancipation Proclamation freeing the slaves in the interest of humanity.[16] Woodrow Wilson ran on a platform which limited the President's tenure to a single term, yet he sought and secured renomination and re-election.[17] His friends promised that he would keep the

15 *World Almanac*, 1945, 724, 725.

16 James Garfield Randall, *Constitutional Problems Under Lincoln*, D. Appleton-Century Company, New York, 1926, 56-59.

17 C. E. Merriam, *Four American Party Leaders*, The Macmillan Company, New York, 1926, 49-50: "You can build a flimsy platform and stand on it successfully, provided its basis is in the right kind of spirit" (quoting *Writings*, II, 418).

United States out of war before his second election; however, after the election, he recommended that the nation should enter the worst war to which the United States had ever been a party. He was guided and controlled in each instance by imperative events. Therefore, to those who denounced President Roosevelt for ignoring his pre-election promises to curtail expenses, the President could have rejoined that to have to do so would have been a crime against humanity in the light of the existing situation.

In the 1936 campaign, Governor Landon, the Republican candidate, had much to say about the President's failure to keep his promises. At the same time he indulged more profusely in pre-election promises than any other presidential candidate in the history of this country; he averred, for example, with the solemnity of a religious vow, that if elected, he would keep his promises. Then he promised to reduce taxes, curtail the budget and pay off the debt, take care of the unemployed, remedy the generations-old complaint of the farmer, conserve the eroding soil, provide security against old age and the hazards of industry, compose the conflict between capital and labor, bring about recovery and set the nation to rights.[18] A single citation will show how Governor Landon kept his promises while chief executive of the state of Kansas. The following excerpt is taken from the *Afro-American* of October 3, 1936.

> ATCHINSON, KANSAS—Dr. D. L. Stewart, leading physician of this city, has taken the lead in organizing "Roosevelt for President" clubs as a rebuke to Governor

18 Speech delivered by Alfred M. Landon in Columbus, Ohio, quoted in the *Chicago Tribune*, October 12, 1936, 2. Also, speeches at Philadelphia, on October 27, and at Madison Square Garden, New York City, on October 29.

> Landon for his failure to keep his promises to eradicate discrimination from the Kansas University Medical School.

In a statement to the *Afro-American* Dr. Stewart, who prior to Governor Landon's second term was an ardent Republican, declared that he would not have opposed Governor Landon if the latter had merely failed to take those steps as a matter of course. But, declared Dr. Stewart:

> While he was campaigning for election the first time I invited him to my private office and had him confer with ten leading colored Republicans of the community. At that meeting we told him of the conditions which existed at Kansas University Medical School. He expressed surprise, and gave us his word that if elected, he would correct that evil. It was only upon his promise that we went to work and put him over.

A little further Dr. Stewart continued:

> After two terms of office conditions at the University of Kansas are not only the same, but are growing worse each year and Landon refuses to lift a hand. This is only one of the charges we have against him, but I cite this merely because it involves a definite promise and proves him to be a man who will not keep his word to colored voters.[19]

Following the publicity which the Negro press gave to the

19 *Afro-American*, October 2, 1936.

exposure—such publicity is in its own right significant—several of the leaders of Negro thought began to speak for President Roosevelt's re-election against Governor Landon. Professor Kelly Miller, a scholar of no mean repute, wrote several articles under the title, "Why the Negro Should Vote for President Roosevelt." These were released by the Associated Negro Press for public consumption.[20] In some articles he made a careful comparison of the programs and philosophies of the two candidates as well as the platforms on which they were campaigning; in one article his analysis led to the conclusion that Landon was "nothing but negatives as far as the good of the Negro is concerned, while Roosevelt is an accumulation of positives for their best interests."[21] His article of October 11 was especially strong. In it he pointed out with great skill and clarity how a vote for Landon was a vote against the Negroes' best interest. His language here is sufficient in itself for the matter at hand.

> During the free silver craze when the western Republicans combined with the southern Democrats to kill the Federal Election Bill in exchange for the support of free silver, John M. Langston (colored Representative from Virginia) declared that they had crucified the Negro for thirty pieces of silver. Today the Republican party has shifted its position from the advocacy of strong federal government to that of defender of states rights unmindful of the incidental sacrifice of the Negro by the exchange.

After this assertion he had much to say about the exchange

20 *Chicago Bee,* October 4, 11, 18, 25, 1936. Also, *Pittsburgh Courier,* October 5, 12, 19, 26; *Kansas City Call,* October 5, 12, 19 26.

21 *Chicago Bee,* October 4, 1936.

of the position of the Republicans and the Democrats, the causes for it and the consequences of it; he declared,

> The Democratic party historically stood for local sovereignty as expounded by Calhoun, the Negro's arch enemy and the premier defender of human slavery. It was to fight that pernicious doctrine that the Republican party was founded . . . The Republican party cannot expect the Negro to follow in its recreancy [cowardly policy] . . . Surely the Negro cannot be expected to stultify his intelligence or stupefy his conscience at the behest of the G.O.P., which once meant the "Grand Old Party." Although political exigencies may require him to change his political affiliations, he cannot change his political principles.

With eloquent persuasion sufficient to lead to conviction he identified the present-day Republican party with the states rights doctrine and continued:

> What would the return to states rights mean to the Negro? The bulk of the race still resides in the South where the white race has never accepted the intent and purpose of the Fourteenth and Fifteenth Amendments to give the Negro full political and civil equality with other American citizens. Any increase in the power or authority of those states would undoubtedly be used to restrict and curtail the political rights and privileges which they have been constrained to permit the Negro to exercise under compulsion of federal authority.

At that point the keen-minded writer seems to have endeavored to bring the situation close to the non-intellectual voter. He added:

> Suppose the question of relief were left to the southern states. Does anyone believe that the Negro would get his just and equable proportion? Who would expect Alabama, Louisiana, or Mississippi to award the Negro an equal portion with the whites unless under compulsion of federal authority? When the Negro wished to secure an anti-lynch law, or relief from harsh discrimination in travel, or the right to serve on the grand juries, or the obliteration of white primaries, he appealed to the United States Supreme Court, not the courts of sovereign southern states. The Scottsboro boys would have been instantly sent into eternity if the issue had been left to the state of Alabama . . . Let the Negro ponder long and well before he casts his ballot for a candidate or a party which now reverts to the doctrine of states rights which has been the source of his immemorial evils.[22]

The reasons for quoting from this author at such length is because he was not a politician; his motives were altruistic in that he had no personal "axe to grind." As Dean of the Junior College of Howard University, rated as the foremost Negro university in the United States, and as author of several works in the fields of social sciences and mathematics, he not only had economic security, but also security among members of the Negro race in regard to integrity, character, wisdom, and judgment—those gave him security of status. His fight against the election of Governor Landon and the Republican candidates

22 *Ibid.*, October 11, 1936.

because they had joined hands with the believers in states rights philosophy, and his endorsement of President Roosevelt constituted one of the strongest possible Negro vote-getting devices.[23] The truth of this expression is indicated in the fact that his articles were released through the ANP and consequently appeared on front pages of the Negro newspapers. Their appearance on front pages of the newspapers is also significant for such implies sanction of their content by those papers.

One other prominent non-politican among Negroes should be mentioned as contributing to the development of Negroes' political thought in a substantial way—Bishop R. R. Wright, Jr., of the African Methodist Episcopal Church. He urged Negroes to support President Roosevelt because Republicans were responsible for the following: (1) the bread lines; (2) the loss of life-savings; (3) people's inability to send their children to school as a consequence of these losses; (4) the difficulty of obtaining homes to live in, even though Negroes had to pay exorbitant rents; (5) the difficulty of borrowing money from the banks; and (6) the virtual re-enslavement by conditions of peonage of tenant farmers and sharecroppers. After having placed those charges against the Republicans (some of which cannot be sustained) he declared that President Roosevelt and the New Deal were correcting most of those evils. "There has been no president since Lincoln who has stood for justice for all 'the forgotten men' like Franklin D. Roosevelt."[24]

23 Kelly Miller is author of several scholarly works, among them the following: (1) *The Everlasting Stain*, (2) *From Servitude to Service*, and (3) *The Leopard's Spot*. He has also contributed articles, dealing with different phases of Negro life and culture, to several of the best magazines. He was the founder of the Sanhedrin, a movement the purpose of which was to solve the Negroes' civic, social, and political problems in America by education and peaceful means.

24 *Chicago Bee*, November 3, 1940.

The previous pages have shown how the Roosevelt Administration or the "New Deal" attracted into its fold Negroes in every walk of life—those on relief in cities, farmers, domestic workers, professional politicians, college professors, and some high church officials. If the situation had stopped there, it would have been far short of opening the doors of democracy wider than they had been opened before. These considerations make it necessary to find out what else was done, if anything, to raise the status of the Negro to that of a full American citizen.

In support of President Roosevelt in the campaigns of 1932, 1936 and 1940 the Negro had acquired a new knowledge of his political importance in the United States.[25] The arguments for a reduction of the number of representatives in Congress from the South as was stipulated in the Fifteenth Amendment had about ceased. The Negro was still disfranchised in the South for all practical purposes—eight states by a state-wide rule barred them from participating in the nominating process under the white primacy.[26] The Negroes in the North had not been sufficiently concentrated until after 1920 to get elected to national offices; however, they renewed their efforts to obtain local and state offices by election. Between 1932 and 1940, however, the following states elected the following Negroes to their legislatures, thereby giving the Negro recognition and deference.[27]

25 See Chapter I, which contains a detailed account of this point.

26 In 1930 those states were: Alabama, Arkansas, Georgia, Louisiana, Mississippi, South Carolina, and Virginia. See Monroe N. Work, *The Negro Yearbook,* 1937-38, 103-4.

27 These data are compiled from leading Negro newspapers, especially the following: *Chicago Defender, Pittsburgh Courier, Amsterdam News, Kansas City Call,* and *Baltimore Afro-American,* June-December, 1932-36. Also, Monroe N. Work, *The Negro Yearbook,* volumes for 1932-37.

Negro Members of the State Legislatures and Their Party Affiliations in 1943

State	*Name of Person Elected*	*Political Party*	*City From Which Elected*	*House or Senate*
Illinois	Harris B. Gains	Republican	Chicago	House
	William E. King	Republican	Chicago	Senate
	Warren B. Douglass	Republican	Chicago	House
	A. H. Smith	Democrat	E. St. Louis	House
	C. J. Jenkins	Republican	Chicago	House
	William A. Warfield	Republican	Chicago	House
	Ernest A. Green	Republican	Chicago	House
	Richard A. Harewood	Republican	Chicago	House
Indiana	H. J. Richardson	Democrat	Indianapolis	House
	R. V. Stanton	Democrat	E. Chicago	House
	M. A. Talley	Democrat	Gary	House
Kansas	W. M. Blount	Republican	Kansas City	House
	William H. Towers	Republican	Kansas City	House
Kentucky	Chas. W. Anderson	Republican	Louisville	House
Michigan	Charles Diggs	Democrat	Detroit	House
Nebraska	John Adams, Jr.	Republican	Omaha	House
New Jersey	J. M. Burrell	Republican	Newark	House
	F. S. Hargraves	Republican	Newark	House
	G. R. Moorehead	Democrat	Newark	House
New York	James Stevens	Democrat	New York City	House
	William T. Anderson	Democrat	New York City	House
	Robert W. Justice	Democrat	New York City	House
Ohio	R. P. McClain	Democrat	Cincinnati	House
Pennsylvania	J. W. Harris, Jr.	Republican	Philadelphia	House
	S. B. Hart	Republican	Philadelphia	House
	J. C. Asbury	Republican	Philadelphia	House
	Hobson Reynolds	Republican	Philadelphia	House
	Marshall Shepard	Democrat	Philadelphia	House
	W. K. Jackson	Republican	Philadelphia	House
	H. S. Brown	Independent	Pittsburgh	House
	E. F. Thompson	Democrat	Philadelphia	House
	S. D. Holmes	Democrat	Philadelphia	House
	J. H. Brigerman	Democrat	Philadelphia	House
	William Allman	Democrat	Philadelphia	House
West Virginia	Stewart A. Calhoun	Republican	Keystone	House
	Fleming Jones	Democrat	McDowell Cty.	House

During the period 1932-1936, there were thirty-seven Negroes elected to state legislatures: twenty-one on Republican tickets, sixteen Democrats and one Independent. This is highly significant politically inasmuch as Negroes were elected to office running on the Democratic ticket in several border states. One is almost tempted to speculate relative to what would happen in regard to political alignments if that policy continued in the future. The picture since 1936 is more convincing that the Negro had turned his attention from the Republican party as his savior. Notice the Negroes elected to state legislatures since 1936. For convenience the alphabetical order is used:[28]

Negro Party Membership in State Legislature Since 1936

Name	*State*	*City*	*Party*	*House or Assembly*
C. W. Anderson	Kentucky	Louisville	Rep.	H
W. T. Andrews	New York	New York City	Dem.	A
John H. Brigerman	Pennsylvania	Philadelphia	Dem.	H
R. L. Brockenbour	Indiana	Indianapolis	Rep.	Senate
H. S. Brown	Pennsylvania	Pittsburgh	Dem.	H
Daniel Burrows	New York	New York City	Dem.	H
Charles C. Diggs	Michigan	Detroit	Dem.	H
C. K. Gillespie	Ohio	Cleveland	Rep.	H
W. H. Grant	Indiana	E. Chicago	Rep.	H
E. A. Green	Illinois	Chicago	Rep.	H
A. F. Hawkins	California	Los Angeles	Dem.	A
J. S. Hunter	Indiana	E. Chicago	Dem.	H
H. E. Jacks	New York	New York City	Dem.	H
C. J. Jenkins	Illinois	Chicago	Rep.	H
E. F. Thompson	Pennsylvania	Philadelphia	Dem.	H
W. H. Towers	Kansas	Kansas City	Rep.	H
Rev. D. D. Turpeau	Ohio	Cincinnati	Rep.	H
W. J. Warfield	Illinois	Chicago	Rep.	H

This list shows there were as many Negro Democrats elected to the different state legislatures between 1936-1940 as there were Republicans; during the period each party acquired eight additional seats.

The number of Negroes elected to city councils would not be very revealing in this study because in many of the larger cities the city charters stipulate "the election shall be non-partisan"; however, we find the Democratic strongholds have a larger list of Negroes than the Republican strongholds.[29] The inference is,

28 Florence Murray, *The Negro Handbook,* 159 (compiled from Negro newspapers).
29 *Ibid.,* 160.

more Negroes were being elected to the city councils when they were known or thought to be Democrats.

The appointive offices which have been given to Negroes in this period, 1932-1940, cover a variety of fields ranging from one Federal judgeship—Judge William H. Hastie (succeeded by Judge H. E. Moore)—to several aides, attorneys, assistants, specialists, directors, and analysts in nearly every agency which was established by the New Deal.[30] (The name of the office and the officer is given by Florence Murray in her excellent work).

This partial list of data leads one to the conclusion that the Democratic party was far more considerate of the Negro's interest since 1932 than was the Republican party. The situation was not then (1932-1940) ideal, for anyone who followed the doings in Congress and the pronouncements of certain responsible officials would know that there were still many Democrats who were as bitterly opposed to the Negro in this period as ever before—Bilbo, Rankin, Caraway, Smith, Talmadge, and George, just to name a few of them. The trend seems, however, to have been toward a more tolerant attitude in the South, while in the North definite effort was made to keep the Negro in the Democratic fold.[31]

Considerable space and time might be used in showing how some policies of the Democratic party, which has great strength in the South, still oppose racial justice. It would be difficult to find a Federal agency under the New Deal which has not practiced racial discrimination and segregation in some form. As proof one need only notice the administration of the alphabetical agencies mentioned earlier in this work. It was a Democratic Congress which made it difficult to pass anti-poll tax and anti-

30 *Ibid.*, 154-57.

31 Virginius Dabney, *Below the Potomac,* D. Appleton-Century Company, New York, 1942, Chapters 1-4.

lynching bills in the lower house and impossible to pass them in the upper chamber; it was also a Democratic administration, although the Secretary of the Navy was reputedly Republican, which denied Negroes rank in the Navy at the beginning of World War II. Therefore, despite the fact that Negroes have gone into the party in large numbers, it is not at all certain that they will remain. This is all the more probable since the party has no appealing leadership today, 1951, as it had when Negroes entered in such large numbers in 1932.[32]

It would be grossly incomplete were this chapter to ignore the nomination and campaign of Wendell L. Willkie. In 1940, the Republican Convention, meeting in Philadelphia, nominated for the presidency Wendell Lewis Willkie, formerly of Indiana. He, at the time (1940) was a resident of New York City. He had never held public office, but had shown considerable ability and skill as a business executive when president of the Commonwealth and Southern Corporation, a public utility. He was what is generally called a "Wall Street" candidate and for that reason was thought by many to be opposed to most of the New Deal reforms.[33] The assumption was unfounded, however, as his acceptance speech at Elwood, Indiana, and other activities later showed. In fact, he swallowed the New Deal almost whole, rejecting only the parts that penalized business.[34]

Prior to 1935, he had been consistently a Democrat in his politics, but partly because of the New Deal policy toward big business he had ceased to be a member of that party and seems

32 The writer is cognizant of his not being a historian in the above assertion.

33 *Chicago Times*, S. E. Thomason, publisher, Chicago, issues from October 27 to November 6, 1940, especially the November 3d issue.

34 Freda Kirchwey, "Wendell L. Willkie's Acceptance Speech," *The Nation*, New York, Volume XV, 1940, 144-45.

to have become an independent. After 1935, consider his own expression:

> Why should I for the sake of conformity catalog myself under one of two labels when neither suits me? My political philosophy agrees with neither that of the New Deal nor that of the Republicans as advanced by their leaders. I will not be a liar.[35]

At best, he was a recent accession to the Republican party when he was nominated for the presidency in 1940.

Any discussion of his early life and political philosophy would have significance in this writing only insofar as they attracted or repelled Negro support.

For this reason, both are sketched. He was born in Elwood, Indiana, a small town in which there hung a sign in large letters, "Nigger, don't let the sun go down on you here."[36] This sign had been there for years and was not taken down until the day Wendell L. Willkie was nominated. The fact that he was neither mayor of the town nor the holder of any public office could not be used as a convincing argument to prove his disapproval of it. Many Negroes were of the opinion, since his father was one of the leading citizens there, that he or his father could have done something about it if either had wanted to. To do nothing or to remain silent about such a matter was tantamount to endorsing it or to sanctioning it.[37] Willkie himself had previously shown an intolerant attitude toward the Negro, at least on one occasion. He was charged with always insisting upon the fact that he was a white man. The following incident is offered in proof: Once, a newspaperman approached him for

35 *Current History,* February, 1940, 21-22.
36 *Chicago Bee,* November 3, 1940.
37 *Ibid.,* November 10, 1940.

an explanation of something he had written, which was not in keeping with good democratic practice, nor to the best interest of the Negro, and his only defense for the insult to the Negro was concluded in that expression, "I am a white man." Mr. Rainey, the newspaperman who relates the story, concluded the expression spoke for itself relative to his attitude toward the Negro:

> Mr. Willkie is a white man who wants emphatically to impress you. I am firmly convinced that he would be a white man's president and a white man's president alone (if he were elected.)[38]

The Negro's attitude toward Mr. Willkie was affected unfavorably by the anti-Negro sign displayed in his home town and by his insistence that he was a white man. To many, this insistence implied that he felt himself under no moral obligation to justify anything he had said about Negroes, especially to Negroes, even though such assertions might be regarded by his listeners or readers as unfair and offensive.

It may be repeated for emphasis that the Negro in 1940 had come to identify his interests largely with those of the New Deal, which was in a sense liberal. Mr. Willkie was definitely pro-big business and at least inclined toward conservatism. His philosophy was then a philosophy which many Negroes interpreted as being contrary to their continued civic and political progress. Thus, Bishop R. R. Wright declared, "There is no hope for Negroes in Willkie's candidacy."[39]

In spite of the anti-Negro sign in his home town and the claim of his intolerant attitude Mr. Willkie was far more pop-

38 *Ibid.*, November 3, 1940.
39 *Chicago Defender*, November 4, 1940.

ular with Negroes than the Republican standard-bearer of 1936. There seem to be two basic reasons for it: (1) Willkie adopted many of the New Deal reforms and policies and (2) Negroes were made to feel that President Roosevelt's efforts to obtain a third term implied a dictatorship for America. Such orators as Roscoe Conklin Simmons and Patrick B. Prescott, and Reverend-Attorney Archibald C. Carey made much ado over the suffering of minorities wherever dictators reign.[40] So the adoption of a liberal platform and Roosevelt's third-term aspirations were, at least partly, responsible for the increase of Willkie's popularity over that of Mr. Landon in 1936. In Negro districts of such cities as Chicago, Cleveland, Detroit, St. Louis, Kansas City, and Philadelphia the votes for the two candidates—Willkie and Roosevelt—were pretty well balanced.[41] The votes of the nation as a whole show Willkie to have been far more popular than Landon had been four years earlier; Willkie received 82 electoral votes as compared to Landon's 8 and Willkie's popular vote was 22,237,266 as compared to Landon's 16,679,538.[42] President Roosevelt's popular vote was about the same in each election—in 1936, 27,476,673; in 1940, 27,443,466—but there was a Republican increase for the entire nation of 5,725,172. Prior to 1932, those areas in the northern cities where Negroes live and vote had consistently gone Republican, with the exception of a few districts in New York City and Boston. The nomination on a Republican ticket meant that the area in those northern cities in which Negroes dwelt were safe for Republican candidates.

40 *Pittsburgh Courier*, October 27, 1940; also, *Chicago Defender*, November 4, 1940.

41 "How the Negro Voted in the Presidential Election, 1940," editorial in *Opportunity*, December, 1940;for a particular city—for example, Detroit—see E. H. Litchfield, "A Case Study of Negro Political Behavior in Detroit," *Public Opinion Quarterly*, Princeton, N. J., June, 1941.

42 *World Almanac*, 1945, 746-47.

But in 1936, they went strongly for the Democrats; in 1940, they balanced between Republicans and Democrats, thereby paving the way for the Negro as an independent in politics, a development which will be discussed in the next chapter of this study. That chapter will be short but significant since both Willkie and Roosevelt are now dead and the loyalty of the Negro to their respective parties was somewhat influenced by the personalities of those men.

CHAPTER VI

The Negro: Independent of Party Labels

The findings recorded in this chapter are the results of a careful study of the trends in the political responses and behavior of the Negro since 1932. An effort is made to record in a scientific way what has taken place in the political thought of the Negro—not what ought to have taken place. His position today, that is, independent of party labels, is of such recent date that only trends in the direction of independence can be documented. The paucity of documents, however, does not mean a paucity of reason. On the contrary, there is abundance of reason for the independence of the Negro to party labels today. Reason is given in support of all assertions, many of which are not documented; however, many of the assertions are the result of observations and analysis.

The Negro found himself after 1936 in the best position, politically, he had ever known in this country. His bolt of the Republican party in 1932, his wholesale support of the Democratic ticket in 1936, his divided support between the Republican and the Democrat in 1940, the nomination of James Ford, a Negro on the Communist ticket for the Vice-Presidency in 1936, are among the incidents which brought forcibly to his mind the fact that voting, the use of the elective franchise, should be a sensible act, not an emotional one. Attachment on the basis of sentimenality, therefore, had to be discarded to make place for rationality. Issues and men had become far more important than party labels. That position made both parties hear him when he spoke, and make worthwhile bids for his support. Both of the major parties—the Republicans who repudiated him, and the Democrats who did not want him—have had, since 1936, a sense of security when they could count on the Negro's support. His independence had given him new freedom.

None doubt that freedom is spiritually and physically invigorating. The United States of America is a land in which men are free or have hope for freedom. It was in a quest for freedom that the nation had its inception; and since its birth, it has been blessed with a large number of truly great men who have made substantial and powerful contributions to the concept of freedom.[1] The phenomenal growth of the country and its spectacular development are testimony to its spiritual and physical vigor. All segments of the population of this promised land found their functions and their places, and made their contributions to its now undoubted genius, power and prominence. Of all these, the Negro segment feels aggrieved that it too is not now a fully accredited and participating member in the blessings and benefits, duties and responsibilities which American citi-

1 The list is a long and imposing one, embracing men in the fields of letters and religion, as well as in politics or statecraft.

zenship ought to confer.[2] Instead, he finds himself with something less than full citizenship.[3] He finds himself a minority problem, with all that the term connotes, in a land in which philosophically and doctrinally such a thing can have no existence. The fact that it does exist and that it is inconsistent with the delineations of the American dream is the creation of the problem.

The so-called Negro problem in America is complex, involved and bewildering. The pattern of Negro life and thought in respect to the over-all national pattern is in a state of constant ferment. The differences and changes from area to area and from time to time are confusing, inconsistent, unreasonable, and, at times, disheartening. This lamentable state of affairs, on the one hand, is the result of and is intensified by the Negro's effort to free himself from his submerged position and, on the other hand, the social inertia which flows from the reluctance of the non-Negro to forego traditional attitudes and stereotyped customs. This reluctance is reflected in the determination of too many Americans to maintain the *status quo.* This tug-of-war and struggle for stature occasions in the Negro a welter of emotional disturbances and traumatic experiences, which in turn have stimulated a tremendous assortment of organizations and individuals determined to find a way out of this dilemma.[4] The

2 Rayford W. Logan, editor, *What the Negro Wants,* University of North Carolina Press, Chapel Hill, 1944, Chapter I. Dr. Logan finds the Negro in the United States to be a "third-rate" citizen only, and in many places unable to enjoy the liberties accorded aliens and enemies.

3 *Ibid.,* 6-9.

4 A few cases in point are:

a) The Marcus Garvey Movement, 1920-24. See Freman W. Talley, "Garvey's Empire of Ethiopia," *World's Work,* Volume XLI, 264-67; W. E. DuBois, "The Man, the Merit, and the Movement," *Century,* Volume CV, 539.

b) The "Forty-ninth State" Movement. See *Opportunity,* April, 1938, 106-9; June, 1939, 164 ff.

c) The Negro Congress. See *Chicago Bee,* February 28, 1936.

organizations and individuals pursued different courses, used different techniques, commanded varying amounts of support and enthusiasm, but all were working sincerely to effect an improved status for the Negro in America, even though each had chosen a different facet or "front."

Few, if any, Negroes minimized the importance of the political front. Among those who have worked on it were an ever increasing number of so-called "Independent Negro voters." In those sections of the country where the Negroes had unrestricted access to the ballot, there has been an observable tendency on the part of large numbers of them not to adhere to rigid party affiliations. To arrive at that situation has not been an easy task for those voters. The Negro has had a long history of allegiance to the Republican party, and, for the most part, has affectionately known no other. For years, the Democratic Party label alone was enough to give the Negro voter a "blind spot" in respect to the worth and merit of any candidate or principle of that party. Happily, changes have been wrought in this matter, due in large part to population shifts occasioned by two great wars, the concentration of Negroes in urban and industrial centers of the North, and the power and efficiency of "big political machines" with their broad-gauge policy of appealing to and skillfully harmonizing racial and economic pressure groups.

In theory, the American Negro, like other Americans, is generally regarded in his political affiliations as being a member of one or the other of the two major parties. In fact, he is just that, except that no matter what his formal or announced party affiliation has been, there was always the superadded consideration and acute awareness of race. This consideration and awareness of race is a thing of necessity and not of choice. He has felt, rightly or wrongly, that his unenviable position in the social, political and economic life of the nation requires that he follow a course of action that no other members of the electorate are called upon to do; it requires that he use different yardsticks of measurement, and that his standard for determining excellence and fitness be somewhat out of balance.[5]

In short, the independent Negro voter has believed that he was practicing discriminate judgment when he subjected the party, its platform and its candidates to what he considered the ultimate test, namely: Will the "Negro Cause" be better served by giving his support to this party and its candidates or to some other? The test may be and frequently has been extended to the question of the expediency and wisdom of supporting candidates *in spite* of their parties—a practice that is followed with growing frequency.[6] The charge could be raised that the test does less than full credit to the persons using it, in that it ignores and does violence to the democratic concept. As American citizens exercising the privileges of the ballot, they owe a duty to the republic and their fellow-citizens to support those instrumentalities and persons who by character and fitness have shown themselves best able to serve the whole interest. There can be no quarrel with the statement of the duty as the statement of the ideal. However, the independent Negro voter has rationalized his use of the test, and justified the compromise of the ideal, as the conscious and protective reaction to the social impact of his day-to-day living in a not wholly congenial society.

The independent voter found it necessary to foreswear in large measure the prerequisites, benefits and privileges that might have accrued to one who gave unquestioning loyalty to a party. Irregularity or even no party affiliation was the penalty he had to pay when he was effectively bringing about, according to his

5 *Chicago Bee* of February 9, 1936, gives an excellent account of "The Negro Sanhedrin," organized by Kelly Miller, February 11, 1924. Many points similar to these are carefully discussed.

6 Cf. the four presidential campaigns of Franklin Delano Roosevelt, in 1932, 1936, 1940, and 1944.

convictions and through his use of the ballot, that minimum guarantee of constitutional and human rights to which the Negro was entitled by all standards of decency subscribed to by men who believed in the basic and essential dignity of the human soul.

CHAPTER VII

Summary and Conclusion

1. Summary

The critical consideration which writers in the fields of history and political science have given the democratic concepts recently are voluminous and interesting. These considerations represent fundamental yearning; though they are interesting, they are no different from those of the adventurers who first settled upon the American shores. We have found that the colonists brought with them a philosophy of equality, liberty, justice, the consent of the governed, majority rule, and the supremacy of the law. The lineage of many of these concepts was many centuries old when the colonists reached these lands. On the secular side, some of these concepts could be easily traced back to the state of nature, and, on the sacred side, to the Garden of Eden. But in order to appraise properly the democratic ideals of the colonists, fortunately, we need go no further back than John Locke, who gave a challenging relevancy to some of these concepts in his historic defense of the revolution of 1688.

At least some, and probably many, of the American colonists were students of the works of Blackstone, who wrote many of Locke's concepts into the English common law in his *Commentaries.* It was the *Commentaries* and the Scriptures which tended to give the colonists both the assurance and finality in their democratic beliefs.[1] It is disturbing to speculate what might have happened to the ideals of the colonists if they could have foreseen a future when both the Scriptures and the *Commentaries* were omitted. Solace is found when one realizes that the earliest colonists with few exceptions were all of the same social status, that is, the middle class, and consequently had much to gain and little, if anything, to lose, by insisting upon equality, liberty, justice, consent of the governed, the supremacy of the law, and the doctrine of majority rule. Pioneering conditions tended to confirm them in these notions.[2]

In recent years such men as Sir Henry Maine,[3] Sir James Stephens,[4] and President Nicholas Murray Butler[5] have sought to show that in the early days there was division in the minds of the colonists in regard to the supremacy of liberty or democracy. If the two concepts could not dwell together in peace, the colonists showed by action that equality had to go. For example, they demanded and received self-government at Jamestown in 1616, and in 1636 Cecelius Calvert granted them liberty of conscience in Maryland. Along with these men who may be designated as unfriendly to democracy conceived as equality may be

1 Charles E. Merriam, *American Political Ideas,* The Macmillan Company, New York, 1920, 3-6.

2 Charles M. Andrews, *The Colonial Period of American History* (fourth edition), Yale University Press, New Haven, 1934, 57.

3 Sir Henry Maine, *Popular Government,* J. Murray, London, 1918, 53.

4 Sir James Stephens, *Liberty, Equality, Fraternity,* London, 1874, 205-9.

5 N. M. Butler, *True and False Democarcy,* Charles Scribner's Sons, New York, 1915, 1-30.

listed the brilliant Frenchman, Emile Faguet. In strong and fascinating language he denies the alleged equality of men, contending that it is impossible to destroy either natural or artificial inequality.[6] Happily, there are contemporary friends of democracy who are as quick to defend it as was Faguet to denounce it. For example, E. G. Conklin believes equality is the dearest of the democratic graces;[7] William E. Dodd asserts, "Democracy is equality, economic, political and social in a large measure";[8] W. R. Inge of St. Paul's feels assured that democracy as a form of society rests on the idea of social equality;[9] James Bryce contends that the love of equality is stronger than the love of liberty.[10]

Fairness to all contentions demands the declaration that all contemporary students are not as emphatic in their support of the American concepts of liberty, equality and democracy as those cited above. However, the opposition has not been sufficient to explode the concepts. Long after this country was organized and long after the tyrannical yoke of taxation without representation had been torn asunder, slavery of large numbers of human beings—ranging from 19 per cent of the total population in 1790 to 16 per cent in 1860—was the common practice throughout the country.[11] For 244 years (1619–1863) the institution of slavery had strong supporters in every field of American

6 Emile Faguet, *The Cult of Incompetence,* E. P. Dutton and Company, New York, 1920, 127.

7 E. G. Conklin, *The Direction of Human Evolution,* Charles Scribner's Sons, New York, 1920, 127.

8 William E. Dodd, "The Struggle for Democracy in the United States," *International Journal of Ethics,* University of Chicago Press, Chicago, Volume XXVIII, 1918, 465-84.

9 W. R. Inge, "Democracy and the Future," *Atlantic Monthly,* Atlantic Monthly Company, New York, Volume CXXIX, 1922, 291.

10 James Bryce, *Modern Democracies,* The Macmillan Company, New York, 1929, Volume I, 68.

11 Monroe N. Work, *The Negro Yearbook,* 1937-1938, 244-46.

life; even some ministers claimed that the Bible sanctioned it.[12]

The concept of natural equality was refuted before 1863 and the assertion of equality in America was compelled to take another form. What form could it take? Generally speaking there were two closely connected avenues opened. First, it could change from the assertion of equality as a past or present fact to the declaration of equality as a worthy ideal. Secondly, equality in the abtsract could be supplanted with equality in the concrete. Common-sense observation denies equality in many things: size, endurance, intelligence, ability and capacity, etc. How may equality be made practical? The answer is: Under the law, in access to the democratic processes, in the enjoyment in proportion to ability of the blessings provided by this country.

In the nineteenth century the claims of human equality in America simmered down to three major claims, each more or less specific: first, all men ought to be equal before the law; second, all men ought to have equal access to the suffrage; and third, all men ought to have equality of opportunity. This does not mean to portray that from the beginning in America a struggle had not been waged for concrete equality. In earlier times equality was something other and far more than specific equalities. The fact that equality existed gave moral validity to the claim that the other democratic concepts ought to exist. The emphasis of the early colonists and statesmen was on natural rather than civil equality.

After the Civil War there was a shift in the emphasis: it was put on civil equality rather than natural equality. This change was not only from equality as a fact to equality as an ideal, but also a change in the emphasis of equality as a natural right, to equality as a civil right. This forecast a revolutionary change in

12 W. G. Brownlow and A. Pryne, *Ought American Slavery to Be Perpetuated?* J. B. Lippincott and Company, Philadelphia, 1858, 82.

the American attitude toward slavery. Even if there were no theoretical justification for the destruction of the institution of slavery the practicality of the doctrines of "consent of the governed" would for the most part make the institution unwise. Booker T. Washington put the situation in a nutshell when he declared, "injustice cannot work harm upon the oppressed without injuring the oppressor."[13]

The whole Anglo-Saxon struggle for the democratic concepts was transferred in some degree to America in the political habits of the colonists. These concepts were brought to their highest expression in the declaration of the Fourteenth Amendment that no state shall "deprive any person of life, liberty, or property without due process of law, nor deny to any person within its jurisdiction the equal protection of the laws." Out of the desire to establish and maintain the provisions and guarantees of the Fourteenth Amendment grew an insistence upon the right to vote. The story of this persistent demand and of its steady realization constitutes one of the most conspicuous chapters in the history of American democracy. Starting with a very restricted suffrage the democratic impulse has overcome successively religious barriers, property limitations, racial disqualifications, and sex boundaries. Since the Republican party championed for the Negro emancipation, citizenship, the elective franchise, and in addition showed them deference and toleration, the Negro came to believe the Republicans were the cause of every reform they had witnessed for their betterment. For a very short time the Republicans proved worthy of the confidence imposed in them by Negroes. They helped elect Negroes to high offices in both state and national governments; they appointed Negroes to positions of authority and honor; constructive and beneficial

13 Booker T. Washington, *Putting the Most Into Life,* Thomas Y. Crowell and Company, New York, 1906, 36.

legislation was enacted in the Negroes' interest; and a strenuous effort was made to raise the Negro to a first-rate citizen.[14]

The first period of helpfulness was of short duration (1865–1877) as said above. This was followed by a period of indifference. During the period of indifference several Republican presidents not only ignored the Negro in making appointment to positions of authority and responsibility, but expressed a determination to build up a strong "Lily White" party in the South even if it meant to sacrifice the Negro. The number of Negroes appointed to administrative positions declined, the number elected to Congress decreased, no legislation was enacted for the protection of the freedmen or, if enacted, was not enforced.

From 1890 to 1910 was a period of silence: silence about enforcing the section of the Fourteenth Amendment requiring a reduction of the number of seats a state should have when the vote was denied to its citizens; silence about the revised states' constitutions with their "grandfather clauses" and poll-tax requirements. The intimidations of the Ku Klux Klan and other organizations received no effective check by the Republicans even when the Republicans knew that the program of such organizations was designed to circumvent the provisions of the Fifteenth Amendment. As a result of the indifference and silence, which is interpreted by the Negro as tacit acquiescence, the South was over-represented in the lower house of Congress.

In recent years, due in part to the fact that the 9,000,000

14 Rayford Logan, editor, *What the Negro Wants,* University of North Carolina Press, Chapel Hill, N. C., 1944, Chapter I. Professor Logan gives a brilliant analysis of the position of the Negro in the United States and makes out his status in the United States to be far less than that of a full-fledged citizen. As a result of careful computation and analysis of the prerogatives and liberties of citizens, he finds that the Negro shares about one third of such prerogatives and liberties, and hence is a third-rate citizen.

Negroes who still live in the South have had no voice in determining "who gets what" in national politics a southern representative has had a smaller constituency than one from the North. In 1940, for example, in the ten southern states of Alabama, Arkansas, Florida, Georgia, Louisiana, Mississippi, North Carolina, Oklahoma, South Carolina and Texas, the votes cast for a Representative averaged 44,298, while in the New England states of Connecticut, Massachusetts, New Hampshire, Vermont, Maine, and Rhode Island the votes for a Representative averaged 130,778; in the middle western states of Illinois, Indiana, Iowa, Kansas, Michigan, Minnesota, Nebraska, Ohio, Wisconsin, North Dakota and South Dakota there was an average of 133,543 votes per Representative.[15]

2. *Conclusion*

Suffrage for Negroes is one of the patterns in which the North and the South of the United States are most dissimilar. The question of suffrage was one of the greatest factors of change during the last two generations and had much to do with the migration of over one and a quarter million Negroes to the North from the South. We saw in this study as a result of a careful analysis of various data, and a careful study of the documents, that many persons who were able to speak with authority claimed the Negro's position in the South was precarious and that a change in his political thinking was inevitable.

The political significance of the great migration to the North lay somewhat in the concentration of the Negro in restricted areas thereby making such areas, as it were, a "Black Belt." Politicians who carefully observed group behavior patterns

15 *World Almanac and Book of Facts,* The New York World-Telegram Corporation, New York, 1945, 721-47.

knew the Negro vote in such areas was no mean prize, if it could be captured. The indifference of the Republicans, the selfishness of the Republican leaders, both white and Negroes, when set over against the increasing awareness of the power of the ballot by the Negro and the bids of the Democratic party, caused an increasing number of prominent Negroes to repudiate the Republican party. This repudiation was manifested in New York in 1924 when Negroes sent a white Democrat from Harlem to represent them in Albany; in 1928 there was a more striking manifestation when several of the leading Negro newspapers supported Smith, a Democrat, over Hoover, a Republican; in 1932 Hoover was denounced with such force and eloquence by politicians, pulpit and press that it was generally conceded that he, Hoover, would not carry the Negro vote in the pivotal states of Illinois, Indiana, Pennsylvania, Ohio, and New York.[16]

Politicians fear voters, and when a person is a non-voter he is politically defenseless and no consideration is given to his wants and needs by the people in power. The changing of the dwelling place of over a million Negroes was a cause of a corresponding change in their political thought. Whereas they were complacent in the South they became politically militant in the North; whereas politics was a white man's business in the South, politics was the business of all good citizens in the North; and whereas the primary election was *the* election in the South, the general election is the election in the North.

The Negro's position in the North, therefore, was at least partly responsible for his changed political thought. The great Greek philosopher of Ephesus (Asia Minor), Heraclitus, who lived about 500 B.C., is reputed to have said that all beings were constantly undergoing change. Change seems to be in the very nature of things. As far as man is concerned, life seems to offer

16 *Opportunity*, May, 1932, 141.

only one of two alternatives: first, live, and grow and change; or secondly, die. Heraclitus' observation applies to nations, organizations, movements, races, and individuals. The study of every institution developed by finite man reveals a multiplicity of change in its history. The United States is no exception; she is the result of an endless chain of changes which go back to the economic, political and religious disturbances in the Old World prior to the landing of the adventurous pioneers on these shores. Americans all are therefore changed people—changed minds, changed methods, changed practices, changed loyalties, and changed ideals at times.

In order to prevent misgivings let us hasten to indicate that change is for better or for worse. Before a correct evaluation or appraisal of a change can be made the thing being changed should and must be studied for a long period by persons capable of computing its causes and consequences. The reasons for the Negro changing his political loyalties from the Republican party after 1915 are made quite apparent in this book.

It was impossible for the Negro to join the Democratic party in the South due partly to the attitude of the southerners toward him and partly to the Negro's indifference while in the South to political affairs. The great exodus of Negroes from the South beginning in 1915 gave the Negro an opportunity to be politically important again, both parties bidding for his support. The Democrats' success in wooing him from the Republican party is due in part to the fact that in some of the larger cities where Negroes concentrated the Democrats were usually in power: New York, Boston, and Kansas City. In those cities the theory that the Democrats stood for the *status quo* as opposed to liberal reforms and helpfulness was put to flight and there was a tendency for more and more Negroes to align themselves with the Democrats.

When the Republicans became aware that Negro votes were no longer to be carried in the vest pocket of some particular leader simply because he was a Republican, and when they saw Negroes responding in ever-increasing numbers to the bids of the Democrats, their silence and indifference concerning him turned into articulateness and effort. Planks for his betterment in their platforms were again inserted. A few Negroes began to be elected to a few state legislatures on the Repubican ticket, and there are a few instances in which Negroes were appointed to commanding positions. Thus there was a rivalry between the Republicans and Democrats for the Negro's support.

Beginning in 1932, due in part to the depression, the Negroes' support went strongly for the Democratic party. Men who had been Republicans for over half a century found enough fault with the party to justify them in changing to the Democrats. The Democrats made several promises in the campaign relative to the Negro which they kept. This was one means of keeping the Negro after the Democrats had secured his support. The reform legislation enacted by the Democrats, the administration of the relief agencies with deference shown Negroes, the courageous equalitarian pronouncements of the Democratic President, and the support given to Negroes on the Democratic ticket by the party hierarchy are some of the factors that enter into the changed political thought of the Negro since 1915.

By 1930 the Negro in the North had come to believe that it was an exercise in good citizenship to plant his loyalties under men and measures, not under traditional labels. His quest to attain first-rate citizenship and to promote his interests caused him to migrate from the South and to change his traditional Republican allegiance and become independent as a voter. His independence as a voter raised his political stock due in part, at least, to the bids of the major parties for his support and the universal deference shown him by them. The Communist party, in an effort to capture the Negro's vote, went so far as to nominate a Negro, James W. Ford, for Vice-President in 1932 and 1936 and carried on a vigorous campaign among Negroes for his election.

Resulting from the deference and considerations shown the Negro, he gained a new sense of his political value and importance. While in 1915 and previously he was a Republican and a Republican only, in 1940 he was largely an independent voter, supporting men and measures, not party labels alone.

The Negroes who remained with the Republicans demanded more of the party than ever before: more liberal reforms, more jobs for more people, more consideration in the party council while organizing more resistance to the undemocratic practices of the South. Negroes who supported other parties did so with the commitment from the party's boss that every consideration enjoyed by other American citizens would be placed at the Negro's disposal. Neither of the parties has been able to carry out the promises of their leaders in full, but no one can deny that each of the major parties has been recently far more considerate of the Negro's interest than was true prior to 1932.

Historically, shifts of opinion have operated with an extraordinary degree of regularity. Arthur M. Schlesinger worked out a chart of the periods of change from conservatism to liberalism, starring leftward swings:

* 1)	1765-87	6)	1841-61
2)	1787-1801	* 7)	1861-69
* 3)	1801-16	8)	1869-1901
4)	1816-29	* 9)	1901-18
* 5)	1829-41	10)	1918-31

He based his conclusion on an analysis of what he called the "dominant national mood as expressed in effective governmental action."[17]

One notices that these periods do not lend themselves to any one political party. Parties can be clearly ruled out as the primary energies for bringing about change. Both of our major parties have known their periods of conservatism and of inaction, and have reflected the spirit of these deeper historical cycles. We have noticed protest groups not only among Negroes, but among workers and farmers, all of which have been important in bringing about changes in party allegiance or shifts from right to left. We found ponderable forces at work among Negroes other than former party affiliation and loyalties, but no correlation can be established between what was offered by any political party and the amount of support the party received from the Negro. Schlesinger's conclusion seems to be a correct one. "Apparently the electorate embarks on conservative policies until it is disillusioned or wearied or barred, and then attaches itself to liberal policies until a similar course is run."[18]

Every election upset seems to have marked a unique period of opinion. For example, the time was favorable for a change of policy under Woodrow Wilson's New Freedom, and Franklin D. Roosevelt's New Deal. The intervening Harding-Coolidge-Hoover period gave an atmosphere of a different sort. Thus our history reveals clearly distinguishable periods when accomplishments which at one time could not be made and achieved were at other times attained under other conditions. The era of Jacksonian democracy had its force and flavor. The Reconstruction

17 "Tides of American Politics," *Yale Review,* Yale University Press, New Haven, December, 1939, 220.

18 *Ibid.,* 229.

period reflected a different state of mind, as have also the Progressive period and the New Deal. We are therefore forced to conclude with Crane Brinton that human beings can go only so far and so long under the stimulus of an ideal.[19] Therefore, change is not only going on all the time in all finite things, but it has been a welcome phenomenon since 1915 in the realm of politics by the major parties and the Negro.

One notices that the changed political thought of the Negro has not been to any considerable extent from one extreme to another. He has tended to be moderate in both thought and action. For example, when the Communist party in 1932 and again in 1936 made strenuous effort to gain the Negro's support by nominating a Negro, James W. Ford, for Vice-President, the Negro showed no unusual excitement. A study of election returns in sections where large numbers of Negroes vote indicates that the Communist party was not very popular with Negroes.[20]

The bids of the two major parties for the Negro's support has given him a new sense of his political importance which has made him somewhat of an independent in politics. Independence does not mean that the Negroes are aloof toward the two major parties, but that they are no longer following labels, but men and issues. The Negroes who have remained Republicans have demanded far more of the party in terms of progressive legislation, reforms and deference than they demanded before 1915. There has not only been a change from Republicans to Demo-

19 Crane Brinton, *The Anatomy of Revolution,* W. W. Norton and Company, Inc., New York, 1938, 243.

20 *World Almanac,* 721-47. One may study the returns in such cities as New York, Chicago, Detroit, Cleveland, Philadelphia, Kansas City, Pittsburgh, St. Louis, Cincinnati, Baltimore, and Boston, and find that the districts in those cities where Negroes were concentrated showed little or no vacillation beyond the Democratic-Republican contest. In no city did the Communist ticket poll enough votes to threaten either the Republican or the Democratic party.

crats and to a position of independence, but there has been a change in demands by the Negro upon the party he supports.

Thus the Negro says with Elinor Wylie in her poem entitled "Quarrel":

> Let us quarrel for these reasons:
> You detest the salt which seasons
> My speech; and all my lights go out
> In the cold poison of your doubt.
> I love Shelley, you love Keats;
> Something parts, and something meets.
> I love salads, you love chops;
> Something starts, something stops;
> Something hides its face and cries;
> Something shines, something dies.
> I love blue ribbon brought from fairs;
> You love sitting, splitting hairs;
> I love truth and so do you,
> Tell me, is it truly true?

APPENDIX 1

Questionnaire

1. Age .... Over 21 .... Under 21 ....
2. Sex: Male .... Female ....
3. Residence .... State .... County .... Town ....
4. Were you born in this state? Yes .... No ....
5. Were you born in the North? .... South ....
6. If you were born in the South, do you plan to return? ....
7. If you were born in the South, how old were you when you left? Over 21 .... Under 21 ....
8. Did you leave of your own volition? Yes .... No ....
9. What was the main reason for your leaving?

10. Education: (check highest level reached) Grade School .... High School .... Trade School .... College .... Professional School ....
11. Political Party: Democrat .... Republican .... Independent ....
12. Have you ever paid poll taxes? Yes .... No .... Voted in Primary? Yes .... No .... In state election? Yes .... No .... In national election? Yes .... No .... How many times in either? ....
13. What party did you support prior to 1932? Democrats .... Republicans ....
14. Were you ever prevented from voting? Yes .... No ....
15. Have you ever contested your right to vote? Yes .... No ....
16. Results

17. The answers to questions 7, 8, 9, 12 are exceedingly important in furnishing information needed in a dissertation. Give these questions your immediate attention. In number 16, you may make any additional statement you like.

APPENDIX 2

6505 Langley Avenue
Chicago, Illinois
August 21, 1945

Mr. Elbert L. Tatum
5915 South Michigan Avenue
Chicago, Illinois

MY DEAR SIR:

I am more than ordinarily happy to execute the questionnaire which you sent to me. I am taking time to make additional comments because, first, the problem you are dealing with is one which has been close to my heart for years, and secondly, having been in a politically conscious setting all my life, my father having been a member of the state legislature of Mississippi in my early days; my brother, and I, having led Negro delegations to the national conventions a time or two, makes me somewhat of an authority on certain phases of the Negro's political life. Negroes have been betrayed by the Republicans since 1877 when the federal troops were withdrawn from the South. Since then, the Republicans have not the Negro's vote, but have forgot them in most beneficial matters.

Now as to the questions 7, 8, 9, why I left the South. I left the South not in an effort to make more money than I was making in Meridian, Mississippi, but I left in order that my children might have an opportunity to develop their talents and capacities unhampered and unrestrained by a prejudiced and personality-dwarfing environment. Observation and experience had taught me that the average southern Negro was possessed with an inferiority complex that he would not have had, had he been in a northern environment For a Negro child to be reared in the South in his early and formative years is to take the chance of stifling his mentality and curbing his ambitions. The way to avoid those possibilities was for me to take them away to a place where the doors of opportunity were open to them or at least not tightly shut simply because they are Negroes.

Moving from the South permitted me to pool my resources, mental, spiritual, and material, with other oppressed and suppressed people in the interest of a fuller and nobler life. Thus a man was neither loved nor hated, admired or admonished, because of the political label he wore. My position was not different from thousands of others.

Many additional facts will be given to you when you come over to the office.

Very truly yours,
DR. ELMER E. HOWARD

APPENDIX 3

3501 South Parkway
Chicago 15, Illinois
October 10, 1945

Mr. Elbert Lee Tatum
5915 South Michigan Avenue
Chicago 37, Illinois

Dear Sir:

In addition to executing your carefully prepared questionnaire I am giving my reasons for remaining a Republican:

Sentiment does not sway me in my political affiliations. Nevertheless I am not oblivious to the political history of my country. History reveals to me that the overwhelming part of the colored American's political, economic and social advancement has been made under Republican leadership.

Emotional approaches based upon the service of "Lincoln, the Great Emancipator" and the "Colored Man's Debt to the Republican Party" have negligible influence in shaping my political opinions.

I am a Republican because I am convinced that most of the truly, liberal and sympathetically interested politicians, of the white race, are members of that party. They are not primarily interested in political preferment but have a well-conceived attitude and policy favorable to colored people. Political expediency in Republican attitudes is not nearly so apparent as with the Democrats. I am led into this state of mind because even among northern Democratic circles many prominent Democratic leaders have declared that "This is a white man's country" and that "The colored man must know his place."

It is impossible for me to reconcile myself to the National Democratic party while the solid south is still in the saddle and corrupts and contaminates the philosophy of the body politic. Flagrant evidence of racial attitudes of the respective parties is always evident at the National Conventions. The colored voter is extended almost every courtesy by the Republicans but the Democrats, even there, are unable to conceal their contempt and opprobrium. The reactionary, unreconstructed Bourbon southerners sally above the Mason-Dixon and without fear of rebuke give vent to their intolerance and bigotry.

While in State and local elections, I can see the virtue of the colored citizen offtimes splitting his vote, I have never yet witnessed the occasion when I deemed the time propitious for me or any other colored American to vote the National Democratic ticket.

While I am fully aware that the Republican party is sadly in need of dynamic, liberal leadership, and while I am conscious of the failure of the party to comprehend and understand that the nation has reached the end of an economic and political era, I fully believe that the Republican Party will adapt itself to political and changing social conditions with more intelligence than Democrats.

If your space and my time permitted, much more would be said about the matter. Let this suffice until the extension.

Yours very truly,

JOSEPH D. BIBB

APPENDIX 4

417 East 47th Street
Chicago 15, Illinois
October 8, 1945

Mr. Elbert Lee Tatum
5915 South Michigan Avenue
Chicago 37, Illinois

DEAR SIR:

It was a genuine pleasure to fill out the questionnaire. These other comments will probably be of help to you in your undertaking.

Many political parties have come upon the scene since the establishment of our Country, but it was not until the Republican Party organized and took the reigns of government that we made any progress towards the Nation we are now.

It has been established in our country that we live and exist under a two party system and no more, the Democratic Party and the Republican Party; therefore in choosing your political destiny, one must make up his mind which one of two parties, Democratic or Republican, best represents his ideals and aims.

Some people think that the choice of a political party is by accident, far be it from that. The farmer, the industrialist and the business man from Europe, of the Scandinavian Countries, as a rule are Republicans, while the Irish and the people who come from the Central and Eastern parts of Europe, such as Poland and Bohemia, are Democrats. Thus you see a higher class of foreigners affiliating with the Republicans than with the Democrats.

The chief reason for that is the former were landowners, business men and industrialists who thought they could better protect themselves in the Republican Party here. On the other hand, the people who migrated from Central and Eastern Europe were usually poor and thought they could better reach their objective in the Democratic Party.

The Republican Party offers the only hope for the Negro, that is my reason for remaining loyal to it. The Republican Party believes in high tariff, which keeps a lot of goods by cheap labor from coming into our Country, competing with American goods. Without such protection, cheap labor would lower our standard of living. The Republican Party believes in a strict enforcement of Civil Service laws, thereby giving the Negro his best chance to obtain Civil Service positions.

In studying the two parties one must take into consideration the development of the country under the party, its method of procedure and activity. The procedure of our two party system makes it impossible for the Negro to achieve any great degree of success under the Democratic Party; for instance, since March 4, 1933, the Democratic Party has been in control of our National Government, but not one single piece of legislation has been enacted for them. Through the seniority rule in Congress, the Chairman of every important Committee in Congress is a Southerner who is a Democrat and he makes it impossible to get constructive legislation in the Negro's interest. In fact, it is *to get it* out of the Committees.

The party is always larger than the man; men come and go in both parties, but the principles, issues, and ideals go on. The Republican party's past history on immigration, tariff, Civil Service and labor as well as its efforts at present, all react to the benefit of the Negro, who must to a greater degree than anyone else in this Country, depend upon earning his living and maintaining himself through labor. It is for these reasons I am a Republican.

ERNEST A. GREENE

APPENDIX 5

3507 South Parkway
Chicago, Illinois
October 14, 1945

Mr. Elbert Lee Tatum
5915 South Michigan Avenue
Chicago 37, Illinois

DEAR SIR:

Here is the questionnaire you sent me. I am in addition to your questions attempting to defend my position.

It was about 1915 that the bonds which held the Negro to the Republican party began to dissolve. The bitterness which had existed after the Civil War between white North and white South was disappearing. Closer social and economic ties were bringing them together and the South waged an unrelenting battle to win the North over to its racial credo.

The administration of William Howard Taft when he openly declared that he was forsaking the policy of appointing Negroes to office in southern states against the wishes of the majority of residents there was an open indication that the Republican Party no longer intended to try to build up its party strength in the South through reliance upon Negroes. Various efforts to develop a white, so called "lily-white" Republican party in the South followed. Gradually Negro Republican leaders in the South were superseded as delegates and finally only one Negro national committeeman served as a symbol representing the Negroes in the party and his was admittedly a rotten borough type of representation. Negroes practically disappeared from important federal office-holding.

Gradually big business which used politics after all to maintain its *status quo,* saw that it could make tools of southern senators and congressmen as easily as it could northern. A combination began to develop which is flowering today and finds the democratic southern representatives espousing bills which are representative of the conservative business interests of the North.

In the meantime, the older Negro leadership, which thought in terms of the Republican party and Abraham Lincoln as their saviors from slavery, were dying off. At the same time the descendants of the Union soldiers who fought in the Civil War and the abolitionists of New England were passing. The new generation of Negroes, short lived as to memories, by the time Roosevelt and the New Deal appeared upon the scene developed a totally different brand of political thinking. They made cause with labor and the masses as against the classes whom they previously had served.

The New Deal through appointment of well trained young Negroes to important positions, greater in number if not in degree of importance, captured the thinking of the Negro masses until a district formerly solidly Republican, now is as definitely Democratic.

Yours very truly,

CLAUDE A. BARNETT

BIBLIOGRAPHY

This book is compiled largely from source material which is so abundant and interesting that a person might easily spend an entire life studying it. Secondary materials have been used to reflect contemporary opinions and trends in Negro thought. In nearly every instance where secondary material was used the material was compiled by men of high scholarship and integrity who used original sources and documents. Therefore, the secondary material is reliable whether it represents observation, reason or research.

Both source and secondary materials are arranged in the order of their importance or value for this study. In another study another person might employ considerable portions of these data, but might arrange his data differently, because what is of primary importance in this study might not be of primary importance in another.

No effort is made to list all materials of value used in this study, but only to list those of most value. It is possible that an error is made in listing what follows as most important for so much enters one's subconsciousness when he reads intensely and extensively as to render him at times unaware of its origin, and thus he writes it as his own. What appears therefore to be original may be unoriginal in the sense that at least parts of it entered the mind from ideas expressed or suggested by other persons. With this thought in mind, the writer's consciousness of materials falls into two broad classes: (I) Source, (II) Secondary.

1. Sources

Congressional Record, Vol. 34, pt. 2, 56th Congress, Second Session, also Vol. 37, Second Session, 1866-67, 70-71, 91-92; *Congressional Globe,* 1868, Vol. VL; also the 39th Congress, 1866, Government Printing Office, Washington, D.C., were of unusual value in that they contain accounts of committee reports, debates, speeches, and reports of investigations and subjects involving Negroes. Similar data are found in other volumes, but these volumes contained material indicated in the dissertation in various places. By using materials contained in these documents one is able to judge both the individual and his party's policy in reference to the Negro.

The proceedings of the *National Republican Convention,* 1854-1940, and the minutes of the *National Democratic Convention,* 1876-1940. These data indicate the considerations given to the Negro problem in the national conventions of the two major political parties. Their expressions or silences were valuable in both inference and in making deductions.

William Hickey, editor, *State Papers, Public Documents and other Sources of Political and Statistical Information,* T. K. and P. G. Collins, Philadelphia, Pennsylvania, 1847, contains several documents from which materials were obtained relative to customs, laws and practices in several states and how they affected the Negro both slave and free.

Miscellaneous Documents of the House of Representatives for the Second Session of the 47th Congress, Government Printing Office, Washington, D.C., 1882-83, contains valuable records of the Negroes in Congress; the speeches made by some of them, bills introduced, their participation in debates and discussions, the committees on which they served, and much valuable personal data.

G. Hunt and J. B. Scott, ed., *Debates in the Federal Conventions of the United States of America,* Oxford University Press, New York, 1920, gives a most detailed account of the heated debates between people who supported slavery and those who opposed it; the three-fifths clause, the representation in Congress clause, and several other compromises.

Senate Report on a Portion of the Message of the President, March 16, 1865, contains Lincoln's recommendation of a Freedmen's Bureau for educational development of the Negro.

Frank Moore, ed., *The Parliamentary Debates,* G. P. Putnam Company, New York, 1861, Vol. 168.

W. O. Blake, *The Political History of Slavery in the United States,* Columbus, Ohio, 1857. A compilation of source material published and sold exclusively by subscription. The greatest value of this work in the immediate undertaking lies in the wealth of material on the question of slavery which it contains. It covers every phase of slavery in the United States.

Carter G. Woodson, ed., *The Mind of the Negro as Reflected in Letters written during the Crisis, 1800-1860,* The Association for the Study of Negro Life and History, Washington, D.C., contains letters from several persons. The most valuable for this study were the letters from Frederick Douglass to Mr. Auld and to William Lloyd Garrison.

United States Department of Commerce, *Bureau of the Census, "Reports of Manufacturing Industries in the United States, 1880-1926,"* Government Printing Office, Washington, D.C., helpful data on Negroes in northern industries.

United States Bureau of the Census, "Negroes in the United States" *Bulletin Number 8,* Government Printing Office, Washington, D.C., helpful data on Negro farmers.

Frank Moore, *The Rebellion Record,* G. P. Putnam, New York, 1861, Volumes I and II, is a compilation of events relative to slavery, indicating who said what, when, and how, about the Negro, his rights and duties and prerogatives, thereby revealing the mentality of the time.

William Waller Herring, *Statutes At-Large, being a collection of Laws of Virginia from the First Session of its Legislature in 1619,* Volume II, Richmond, 1819. The value of this document lay in what it says about slaves: manumission and how obtained, children of mixed races and their status, the treatment of slaves, etc.

Helen J. Cotterall, *Judicial Cases Concerning American Slavery and the Negro,* two volumes, Carnegie Institution, Washington, D.C., 1926, was most helpful in revealing the efforts of the Negro to obtain freedom as a slave, and to enjoy his freedom since emancipation. The value of these cases cannot be overemphasized in this study. They reveal that the Negro's faith in the courts was superior to his faith in the legislative or administrative branches of the government.

A. B. Hart and Edward Channing, *American History Leaflets, Colonial and Constitutional,* Parker B. Simmons Company, Incorporated, New York, 1896, is a collection of source material on such questions as the provisions of the Northwest Ordinance, 1784, 1787; the Missouri Compromise, the Dred Scott Decision, the Louisiana Purchase, and several other such topics.

The Census Reports of the Bureau of the Census, Government Printing Office, Washington, D.C., were valuable in determining the growth and decline of the Negro percentage in the population, the trends in Negro migration, their achievements in education, commerce and business and similar questions, 1790–1940.

A. B. Hart, editor, *American History Told by Contemporaries,* The Macmillan Company, New York, 1920, in five volumes, was the account of the thinking of representative citizens on many basic problems in our country.

Monthly Labor Review, Government Printing Office, Washington, D.C., a monthly report on the state of labor by the Census Bureau, was of value in studying the labor movement, 1915–1940, and especially Negro labor in the period.

The World Almanac, New York World-Telegram Corporation, 1940, 1945, was valuable in studying the election returns, thereby indicating the popularity of candidates for office in local, state or national elections.

United States Department of Labor, *Monthly Labor Review,* 1921–1930, valuable for information of where the Negroes went when they left the South in this period.

Thomas Marshall in the *House of Delegates of Virginia on the Policy of the State in Relation to her Colored Population,* January 14, 1832, Richmond, Virginia, 1832, was revealing of Virginia's stand on the question of emancipation of slaves who had become converted.

Congressional Digest, A. G. and N. T. N. Robinson (editors), Washington, D.C., 1931.

Ralph J. Bunche, "The American City, A Negro Political Laboratory", *Government Research Association Proceedings,* 1928, Volume 53, 64 ff.

Stephen B. Weeks, "The History of Negro Suffrage in the South", *Political Science Quarterly,* edited by Faculty of Political Science, Columbia College, New York City, 1893, Volume 9, 672–703.

F. Bishop, "History of Election in American Colonies", *Columbia University Studies in History,* New York, 1879, Volume III, 7–79.

W. E. B. DuBois, "Reconstruction and its Benefits," *American Historical Society,* New York, Volume 15, No. 4.

Robert F. Carson, "The Loyal League in Georgia," *Georgia Historical Society,* Savannah, 1932, Volume 22, Number 2, 125–153.

(Editorial) "Party Rules Excluding Negroes from Primaries", *North Carolina Review,* Chapel Hill, 1922, Volume 2, Number 9, 207–10.

John L. Love, "The Potentiality of the Negro Vote in the North and South," *American Negro Academy Occasional Papers,* 1905, Number 11, (Copyrighted) Washington, D.C.

R. R. Wright, Jr., "What Does the Negro Want in Our Democracy?" *National Conference of Social Workers, Proceedings,* 1919, 139–44.

Moroe N. Work, *Negro Yearbook,* Negro Yearbook Publishers, Tuskegee Institute, Alabama, 1912–1940.

Florence Murray, *Negro Handbook,* Current Reference Publication, New York, 1942–44.

A. B. Hart, editor, *American History Told by Contemporaries,* The Macmillan Company, New York, 1926, in five volumes.

Allen Johnson, editor, *The Chronicles of America Series,* Yale University Press, New Haven, 1921, in XLIX volumes.

Kirk H. Porter, *National Party Platforms,* The Macmillan Company, New York, 1924.

The Negro in Chicago, Chicago Commission on Race Relations, University of Chicago Press, 1921. This is a compilation of the finding of the Chicago Crime Commission which was valuable in indicating problems raised by the increasing numbers of Negroes there.

The Chicago Tribune, Tribune Company, Chicago.

The New York Times, New York Times Company, New York City.

Cincinnati Post, Post Publishing Company, Cincinnati, Ohio.

The New York Evening Post, D. S. Thackrey, Publisher.

2. *Secondary Material*

This material is divided for convenience into two sections: first, Magazines, and secondly, Books; the third source, Letters, are reprinted in the Appendixes.

a) Periodicals and Magazines

Collier's, Collier's–Crowell Publishing Company, New York, 1932. Volume 82, 13. "Who But Hoover" (editorial).

Opportunity, Journal of Negro Life, Quarterly, National Urban League, New York. Articles are listed by either volume or date. The title of the article is given in order to indicate its bearing on this subject.
February, 1927, William C. Matthews, "The Negro Bloc."
February, 1932, 141, "Presidential Polls" (editorial).
March, 1932, "How Should the Negro Vote?" (editorial).
November, 1932, The Republican Ogden L. Mills and the Democrat James A. Farley discuss the programs and policies of their respective parties as they relate to the Negro–propaganda.

January, 1933, "The Negro votes shifted from the traditional alignment of the Republican Party to the Democratic and Socialist Parties" (editorial).

Ibid., "Did the Negro Revolt?"

October, 1936, Earl Brown, "The Negro Vote" (editorial).

December, 1936, 359, "How the Negro Voted in the Presidential Election" (editorial).

Ibid., 321, "The Negro is Becoming Intelligent on the Question of Party Affiliation."

August, 1938, "Mayor Hague and the Negro."

February, 1939, G. W. McKinney, "The Negro in Pennsylvania Politics."

June, 1939, "The Forty-Ninth State Movement" (editorial).

Articles dealing with the election of 1940 appear in the issues of 1941, which are beyond the scope of this study.

The Crisis, The Crisis Publishing Company, Incorporated, New York. Valuable help was received from articles indicated by date and title.

October, 1916, "The Negro Party."

March, 1916, "The Anthony Amendment."

September, 1920, "How Shall We Vote?"

October, 1928, Floyd Keeler, "The Poll Tax."

November, 1928, "How Should We Vote?"

October, 1932, "Why the Negro Should Vote for Hoover."

May, 1936, "Landon and the Negro."

June, 1937, "Political Future of the Negro as a Voter."

October, 1937, "A New Party."

The Nation, The Nation's Press, New York. Help received from this publication is indicated by title and volume.

W. E. B. DuBois, "The Republicans and the Black Voter," June 5, 1920, 757.

"Negroes in the Republican Conventions," Volume 94, 606 ff.

"President Harding and Social Security," Volume 113, 561 ff.

Freda Kirchwey, "Wendell L. Willkie's Speech," Volume 151, 144–45.

(Editorial) "The Lawless Nation," 1929, Volume 129.

(Editorial) "Hoover and the Wheat," 1931, Volume 133.

Political Science Quarterly, edited by Faculty of Political Science, Columbia College, New York, Volume II, 680–86.

James W. Garner, "New Politics for the South," *Annals of the American Academy of Political and Social Science,* bi-monthly, Philadelphia, January, 1910, Volume 35, 172–83.

Journal of Negro History, Association for the Study of Negro Life and History, Washington, D.C., 1940, Volume 25, 152–200.
Volume 17, October, 1922, Henry A. Wallace, "Negro Delegates from South Carolina to Meet Republican Convention."
Volume 2 (editorial), "Negro's Political power in the South."
H. A. Donald, "The Negro Migration," October, 1921, 338 ff.

Harper's Monthly Magazine, Harper and Brothers, New York.
J. C. Hemphill, "The South and the Negro," January, 1909, Volume 53, 10.
Walter White, "The Negro and the Supreme Court," January, 1931, Volume 162, 238–46.
A. L. Harris, "Negro Migration to the North," 1924, Volume 20, 924–25.

Current History, New York Times, Publishers, New York.
Oren Root, "This is Wendell Willkie," Volume 52, 7, 63.
Robert M. Lovett, "Chicago, the Phenomenal City," Volume 31, 328–34.
"American Negro's New Leaders," April, 1928, Volume 28, 56–91.
R. G. Tugwell, "Flaws in the Hoover Economic Plan," 1932, Volume 35.

Literary Digest, Funk and Wagnalls Company, New York.
(Editorial) "The Negro Status Declared by the President," November 19, 1921, Volume 97.
(Editorial) "The Negro Northward Exodus," August 29, 1931, Volume 107, 4.

North American Review, D. Appleton Company, New York. Thomas A. Hendricks, "Retribution in Politics," 1879, Volume 138, 377–384.
Wendell L. Willkie,"Why I believe in America," Volume 48.
J. Q. C. La Mar, "Ought the Negro to Be Disfranchised?" Volume 138.

Silas Bent, "Al Smith: Executive," *The Independent*, The Independent Publisher, New York, 1928, 590–91.

A. C. Edwards, "The Negro Federal Workers," *Howard University Studies in Social Science*, Washington, D.C., 1941, 73–153.

W. E. B. DuBois, "The Man, the Merit, and the Movement," *Century Magazine*, The Century Company, New York, 1923, 539–40.

T. H. Talley, "Garvey's Empire of Ethiopia," *World's Work*, Doubleday, Page and Company, New York, 1920-21, Volume 41, 264–70.

(Editorial) "Fighting for Hoover," *The New Republic,* The New Republic Incorporated, New York, 1920, Volume 22, 3–6.
"Hoover as a Great White Father," *Ibid.,* 223.
"Hoover and the Negro," *Ibid.,* 223.
Michael Gold, "The Communists Meet," Volume 1, 117-19.

T. A. Hill, "Why Southern Negroes Don't Go South," *Survey,* Survey Associates, New York, November 29, 1919; also, "The Negro Memorial on the Rights of Man," May 11, 1918, 163 ff.

Kingsley Morris, "The Negro Comes North," *Forum,* Forum Publishing Company, New York, 1922, 181–90.

Guy B. Johnson, "Negro Racial Movements and Leaderships in the United States," *American Journal of Sociology,* University of Chicago Press, Chicago, Volume 43, 57–71.

Kelly Miller, "The Political Capacity of the Negro," *American Review of Reviews,* Review of Reviews Company, New York, 1910, Volume 42, 351–52.

Ray Stannard Baker, "The Status of the Negro as a Voter," *Ibid.,* 724–25.

James W. Johnson, "The Negro Looks at Politics," *American Mercury,* Alfred A. Knopf Publishers, New York, 1929, Volume 18, 88–94.

L. A. Walton, "Negro in Politics," *Outlook,* The Outlook Company, New York, 1922, Volume 132, 1924, 472–73.

W. B. Conant, "Future of the Negro," *Arena,* Albert Brandt, Publishers, Trenton, New Jersey, 1908, Volume 40, 62–68.

b) Books

This list is not exhaustive, but represents the books which were found most helpful. The specific and frequent references to some of them indicate their value.

Aptheker, Herbert. *The Negro in the Abolitionist Movement.* N. Y.: International Publishers, 1941.

Blake, W. O. *The Political History of Slavery in the United States.* Columbus (Ohio), 1857.

Bontemps, Arna, and Jack Conroy. *They Seek a City.* N. Y.: Doubleday, Doran and Co., 1945.

Brawley, Benjamin F. *A Short History of the American Negro.* N. Y.: The Macmillan Co., 1939.

Bunche, Ralph J. *World View of Race.* Washington, D.C.: Associates in Negro Folk Education, 1936.

Charnwood, G. R. Benson, Lord. *Abraham Lincoln.* London: Constable and Co., 1917.

Dabney, Virginia. *Below the Potomac.* N. Y.: D. Appleton-Century Co., 1924.

Douglass, Frederick (F. A. W. Bailey). *The Life and Times of Frederick Douglass.* Centenary Memorial Subscribers' Edition; N. Y.: Pathway Press, 1941.

DuBois, W. E. B. *Black Folk Then and Now.* N. Y.: Henry Holt and Co., 1939.

———. *Black Reconstruction.* N. Y.: Harcourt, Brace and Co., 1935.

———. *Darkwater.* N. Y.: Harcourt, Brace and Co, 1920.

———. *Dusk of Dawn.* N. Y.: Harcourt, Brace and Co., 1940.

———. *The Negro.* N. Y.: Henry Holt and Co., 1915.

———. *The Philadelphia Negro.* "University of Pennsylvania Studies in Political Economy, No. 14"; Philadelphia, 1899.

———. *The Souls of Black Folk.* Chicago: A. C. McClurg Co., 1940.

Evans, M. S. *Black and White in the Southern States.* London: Longmans, Green and Co., 1915.

Franklin, John Hope. *From Slavery to Freedom.* N. Y.: Alfred A. Knopf, 1949.

Gosnell, Harold F. *Negro Politicians.* Chicago: University of Chicago Press, 1935.

Hare, M. C. *Norris Wright Cuney.* Washington, D.C.: Associated Publishers, 1923.

Hercules, E. L. *Democracy Limited.* Cleveland: Central Publishing House, 1945.

Herskovits, Melville J. *The Myth of the Negro Past.* N. Y.: Harper and Brothers, 1941.

Hildreth, Richard. *Despotism in America: An Inquiry Into the Slave-holding System.* Cleveland: John J. Jewett and Co., 1854.

Hill, T. Arnold. *The Negro and Economic Reconstruction.* Washington, D.C.: Associates in Negro Folk Education, 1937.

Jaquette, Henrietta Stratton. *South After Gettysburg.* Philadelphia: University of Pennsylvania Press, 1937.

Johnson, Charles S. *The Negro in American Civilization.* N. Y.: Henry Holt and Co., 1930.

Johnson, James Weldon. *Negro Americans, What Now?* N. Y.: Viking Press, 1934.

Josephson, Matthew. *The Politicos, 1865-1896.* N. Y.: Harcourt, Brace and Co., 1938.

Kerlin, R. T. *The Voice of the Negro.* N. Y.: E. P. Dutton and Co., 1920.

Locke, Alain LeRoy (ed.) *The New Negro.* Washington, D.C.: Associates in Negro Folk Education, 1937.

Logan, Rayford W. (ed.). *What the Negro Wants.* Chapel Hill: University of North Carolina Press, 1944.

Lynch, John R. *The Facts of Reconstruction.* N. Y.: Neale Publishing Co., 1931.

McKay, Claude. *Harlem: Negro Metropolis.* N. Y.: E. P. Dutton and Co., 1940.

MacMasters, J. B. *History of the People of the United States.* 8 vols. N. Y.: D. Appleton and Co., 1931.

Merriam, George S. *The Negro and the Nation.* N. Y.: Henry Holt and Co., 1906.

Merriam, Charles E. *Four Party Leaders.* N. Y.: The Macmillan Co., 1926.

Miller, Kelly. *The Everlasting Stain.* Washington, D.C.: Associated Publishers, 1924.

———. *History of the World War for Human Rights.* Copyright by A. Jenkins, 1919.

———. *Out of the House of Bondage.* N. Y.: Neal Publishing Co., 1914.

Morton, R. R. *"What the Negro Thinks."* N. Y.: Doubleday, Doran & Co., 1942.

Myrdal, Gunnar. *The American Dilemma.* Vols. I and II. N. Y.: Harper and Brothers, 1944.

Odegard, Peter. *The American Public Mind.* N. Y.: Columbia University Press, 1930.

Randall, James Garfield. *Constitution Problems Under Lincoln.* N. Y.: D. Appleton and Co., 1926.

Rhodes, James Ford. *History of the United States From the Compromise of 1850 to the Era of the [Theodore] Roosevelt Administration.* 9 vols. N. Y.: The Macmillan Co., 1929.

Scott, Emmett J. *Negro Migration During the World War.* "Economic Studies of the War, No. 16"; Washington, D.C.: Carnegie Endowment for International Peace, 1918.

Smith, Samuel Denny. *The Negro in Congress, 1870–1901.* Chapel Hill: University of North Carolina Press, 1940.

Thompson, Edgar T. *Race Relations and the Race Problems.* Durham (N.C.): Duke University Press, 1939.

Umbreit, Kenneth. *The Founding Fathers, Men Who Shaped Our Tradition.* N. Y.: Harper and Brothers, 1941.

Van Deusen, J. G. *The Black Man in White America.* Washington, D.C.: Associated Publishers, 1938.

Warmouth, Henry Clay. *War Politics and Reconstruction.* N. Y.: The Macmillan Co., 1930.

Washington, Booker T. *The Future of the American Negro.* Boston: Maynard and Co., 1899.

———. *My Larger Education.* Garden City (N. Y.): Doubleday, Page and Co., 1911.

———. *The Negro in the South.* Philadelphia. George W. Jacobs and Co., 1907.

———. *A New Negro for a New Day.* Chicago: American Publishing House (copyright by J. E. MacBrady).

———. *Putting the Most Into Life.* Garden City (N. Y.): T. Y. Crowell and Co., 1906.

———. *Up From Slavery.* N. Y.: Doubleday, Doran and Co., 1900.

Wesley, Charles H. *The Collapse of the Confederacy.* Washington, D.C.: Associated Publishers, 1937.

———. *Negro Labor in the United States.* N. Y.: Vanguard Press, 1927.

Wiley, Bell Irvin. *Southern Negroes, 1861–1865.* New Haven: Yale University Press, 1938.

Wilson, Henry. *Rise and Fall of the Slave Power in America.* Boston: Houghton, Mifflin and Co., 1879.

Woodson, Carter G. *The Negro in Our History.* Washington, D.C.: Associated Publishers, 1922.

———. *The Rural Negro.* Washington, D.C.: Association for the Study of Negro Life and History, 1930.